CONTENT FOR EVERYONE

A PRACTICAL GUIDE FOR CREATIVE ENTREPRENEURS TO PRODUCE ACCESSIBLE AND USABLE WEB CONTENT

JEFF ADAMS

MICHELE LUCCHINI

Content for Everyone

A Practical Guide for Creative Entrepreneurs to Produce Accessible and Usable Web Content

Jeff Adams
Michele Lucchini

CONTENTS

INTRODUCTION: WHO WE ARE AND WHY WE WROTE THIS BOOK

EDUCATING companies around the world about web accessibility is the way we both spend most of our working days. We've worked together for over 10 years for a company called UsableNet, which was founded back in 2000.

UsableNet's first product was a tool to help web developers who used Macromedia Dreamweaver and Microsoft FrontPage make websites accessible. Michele was an early employee with UsableNet, and Jeff joined in 2011.

Jeff is the Director of Accessibility Operations and is a Certified Professional in Accessibility Core Competencies (CPACC) by the International Association of Accessibility Professionals (IAAP). Michele is the Vice President of Delivery and Accessibility Operations and has an extensive background in web accessibility. In our roles, we consult with companies large and small from around the world on their efforts to make their websites, apps, and other digital properties accessible.

This book came about because Jeff is also an author and podcaster. Since 2009 he's published gay romances and young adult fiction featuring LGBTQ+ characters, and in 2015 Jeff and his husband created the *Big Gay Fiction Podcast*.

As he created websites for these endeavors, he did everything he could to make the sites accessible with the limited technical skills he had. There's a difference between knowing what needs to be done and knowing how to do it.

As he visited the websites of other creatives, he saw little consideration for the barriers these sites present for people in the disabled community. The oversight likely wasn't deliberate but more a case of not knowing what to do and how to do it.

In passing, Jeff mentioned to Michele that he was considering writing a book on accessible content designed for creatives who are primarily creating digital content on their own—whether it's a website, social media post, podcast, email newsletter, or other digital content. In short order, it became a project to do together.

There are many things that you, as a creative entrepreneur, can do with limited technical know-how to make your content available for everyone.

Our goal is to keep this book simple, as we're assuming that you're not a web developer but someone who knows how to use the website, social media, and email platforms you've chosen.

We want to help you make your content more accessible using the tools you have available. We'll also provide some additional guidance in case you are able to work with a developer or designer on your website and content.

At times, we'll discuss the legal aspects of web and digital accessibility. Please be advised that we are not attorneys and are not providing legal advice in this book or on the

Content for Everyone website. We are simply providing information that's based on our experience in this field.

Thanks for picking this book up and doing your part to make content accessible and usable for everyone, or in other words becoming more inclusive.

WHY ACCESSIBLE CONTENT MATTERS

BECAUSE IT IS the right thing to do!

It also helps you get your message out to everyone, with no exceptions.

Are you an author promoting your latest book?

Are you a podcaster putting the word out about your show?

Are you a painter or sculptor sharing your latest creation?

Are you a musician showcasing a new song?

No matter how you express your creativity and how you put that out into the world, your business relies on connecting with your current and future audiences so they can find out about what you've made and how they can get it.

Accessibility is about being inclusive so that everyone who wants to interact with your content feels included because they can access it in the way that works best for them.

In this day, with all the knowledge and technology that's available, it should be commonplace to find that content is accessible. Sadly, that's not the case. It's more common than not to find inaccessible content.

You can help change that by making sure what you put online is as accessible as possible and encouraging your friends and colleagues to do the same.

Before we get into what you can do, let's review some statistics that help illustrate how important this is.

By the Numbers

Here are statistics about the known disabled population around the world:

- United States: 61 million adults live with a disability. That translates to roughly 1 in 4 U.S. adults.[1]
- Canada: 6 million, or 22% of Canadians aged 15 and over.[2]
- United Kingdom: 14.6 million, or 22% of adults.[3]
- European Union: Approximately 100 million, or 20% of adults.[4]
- Worldwide: More than 1 billion, or approximately 15% of the world's population, live with some form of disability.[5]

Regardless of the country or region, between 15 and 25 percent of the population lives with some form of disability.

These numbers do not include people who have a temporary impairment. Consider someone who broke their wrist and can't use a mouse. They might have to navigate their computer with a keyboard only. Or someone who wears glasses and lost them. Until they got a new pair, they might need to use a screen reader or some type of screen magnification to engage with text.

There are also situational impairments to consider. These

are things that happen only in certain situations but can impact the ability to use digital content. For example, someone might need to activate captions to engage with a video if they're in a crowded place and don't have earphones for private listening. If someone is outside in the sun, glare might obscure their phone screen, so they might activate the phone's screen reader to help them read text on the screen.

Don't forget there can also be episodic impairments. Consider how a migraine, severe arthritis, vertigo, or other types of flare-ups can impact how someone interacts with the world and digital content.

The number of people with disabilities also increases as the population ages simply because as people age, they are more likely to become disabled.

Internet users are also older than ever before, especially since the COVID-19 pandemic forced many activities online, and therefore seniors have had to become more web-savvy. Now the internet is widely used by all ages to have easier access to goods, services, and content.

As these disability statistics explain, there are many people who may not be able to interact with the content you're creating. If your website and digital communications aren't created with accessibility in mind, you might not be connecting with someone who would love your creations.

Four Primary Disability Types

One of the major myths we routinely debunk is that accessible content means that it's available to blind people who navigate with screen readers. While people who are blind and visually impaired are among the groups to consider, it is not the largest.

Here are the four primary disability types, and the percentage of adults in the U.S. who live with the disability.[6]

Mobility: This is the largest group at 11.1%. Mobility impairments include cerebral palsy, muscle and joint conditions such as arthritis, and paralysis to name a few.

You may not think that a mobility impairment can cause trouble using a website; however, consider severe arthritis that might prevent someone from being able to hold and use a mouse or to tap on a screen accurately.

Cognitive: This is the next largest group at 10.9% of the U.S. adult population. Cognitive impairments include autism, any issues with text, math, or visual processing, and attention deficit hyperactivity disorder (ADHD) to name a few.

Things that can be difficult for people in this group include anything on a site that moves automatically—a carousel, a video, an animation—because it could be a distraction. Someone with dyslexia might have trouble if you're using fancy, curly fonts as it may be more difficult for them to identify the words.

Auditory: Some form of hearing loss is present in 5.7% of the population. This group is key for anyone creating audio content as you must make it available in another format— transcripts and/or captions—so anyone can consume and enjoy it.

Visual: This group is 4.9%. Blindness, low vision, color blindness, and other forms of vision loss impact the way people perceive content. For the blind, screen readers— including text-to-speech tools and braille monitors—allow them to navigate digital content.

For those with vision loss, they rely on content being displayed with proper color contrast and that color isn't the only way important information is presented, among other things.

Of course, it's quite possible that people may have more than one disability, such as someone who may have low vision and ADHD or someone who may have hearing loss along with tremors in their hands.

The possible combinations are numerous, and in each case how someone navigates websites could be different, so it's important to consider content accessibility from that understanding as well.

In addition, there may be members of your audience who use alternative ways to access content because it works best for them. For example, while screen readers are primarily used by those who have visual impairments, someone with dyslexia may use one as they're visually reading text on the screen to help ensure they understand. Someone who has no hearing loss may read a podcast transcript rather than listen to the show because they may comprehend better when reading rather than listening.

The information we give you in the "Practical Guide" section takes these scenarios into account. You'll find that we indicate how each type of impairment benefits from accessible content.

ACCESSING CONTENT ON
THE WEB

IT's no surprise there are many ways to access digital content through a website, an app, social media, and email. Think about the technology you own and how you use it. The most common items include:

- A desktop or laptop computer that is navigated with a mouse, trackpad, or another pointing device.
- A tablet, which is navigated by tapping and swiping the screen.
- A mobile phone, which is also interacted with by tapping and swiping.

In addition, there's also assistive technology that can be used to interact with the digital content. "Assistive technology" is a term often used to describe anything that is used to increase, maintain, or improve the functional capabilities of the person using the technology.[1] Assistive technology helps people who have difficulty moving, speaking, typing, writing, remembering, pointing, seeing, hearing, learning, and so on. Different disabilities require different assistive technologies.

Most computers, tablets, and phones, especially ones using a recent version of the operating system, have assistive technology options built into them that can be configured and used as needed.

Examples of this include:

Screen reader: A text-to-voice technology that can read the on-screen text, read announcements that pop up on screen, and provide descriptions of visual content such as images.

Zoom: Adjusts the size of what's on the screen.

Display features: Allows the user to invert and adjust colors (such as "dark mode"), improve color contrast, reduce motion, help the user find the mouse pointer, and differentiate elements without the use of color.

Screen flash: Used to indicate an audio alert.

Convert to mono: Plays stereo audio as mono to help users with hearing impairments.

Voice control: Allows controlling the device with voice commands.

Controller customizations: Adjusts the mouse, keyboard, and other controllers to behave in the best way for the user.

We encourage you to explore the accessibility settings on the devices you use so that you can understand what it means to use them. You'll typically find them in the general settings for your computer, tablet, or mobile phone. Within settings these are usually labeled as "Accessibility," "Accessibility Features," or "Ease of Access." Some of these features take time to learn how to use efficiently, but they are useful to know so you understand the accessibility of your website and the content you're posting across the web.

How well assistive technology works can be impacted by

the structure of your website and the content you publish, as well as your content in emails and social media posts.

Different People, Different Approaches to Content

Everyone has unique preferences for accessing digital content, which include choices like the device used, the software and apps, the platforms they interact with, and other variables. For people with disabilities, they may use additional technologies as we noted, and how they access—and if they access—content can be impacted by how that content is presented.

We spoke with four people to help you understand how the choices you make when you create content can affect how it's accessed. Keep in mind, each of these people represents a unique example. While their experiences may be the same as others, there may also be differences.

Joe DiNero

We work with Joe at UsableNet where he is the lead of the user testing team that tests websites and mobile apps for accessibility. He's also an assistive technology specialist at Helen Keller Services for the Blind, a nonprofit organization that offers a wide range of services and programs for people of all ages who are blind or have vision impairments. As part of his work with Helen Keller Services, Joe teaches people who are blind or visually impaired how to use assistive technology to aid them in becoming more independent.

Joe is legally blind, having lost his sight as an adult. While he still has some vision, he relies on a screen reader when using websites, apps, and reading email. He's a big music fan, keeping up with bands on their websites, and he also moderates several Facebook groups that focus on music.

Joe told us about what affects his ability to interact with and consume content effectively.

Headings: "I can't tell you how many sites where you get to the home page and there is a ton of material on the page but not one heading on it," Joe says. "That takes away one of my main navigation tools."

While you may have bold text that's designed to designate a heading, that will only be available to someone visually engaging with the site. Unless headings are created correctly, they won't be available to assistive technology like a screen reader.

Links and interactive elements that are not labeled well: Links that are not labeled, such as those with linked images, or a page that is full of "click here" links make navigation more of a challenge. In those instances, Joe says he then must read through all the content to determine where the links will go, rather than getting the information from the link itself.

Keyboard interactions: Being able to operate buttons, links, and other components can be a significant barrier, especially to purchasing something.

"This happens a lot with smaller sites," he says. "The product pages sometimes don't have buttons that interact well with the keyboard, and so it can be difficult to purchase something."

Alternative text for images: It's important, especially when making a purchasing choice, that there's alternative text to describe the image and its function within the context of the page so that people who can't see the image understand what they're buying.

Another area for alternative text is if there is text that's part of an image. "If someone's got a review of their concert in an image, the alt text becomes very important. If it just says 'image of text' [or there's no alternative text or it's wrong], that doesn't really do a lot for me."

Alternative text for images is important on social media as well. "With the Facebook groups I moderate, you'll get the posts that say, 'today on my playlist is this…' and it's three images that are all album covers. Facebook will generate automatic alternative text and say something like 'picture of four people.'

"For me to even attempt to figure out what the poster is listening to, the only thing I have is the comments if somebody says the band name or a song from the album. It would be a totally different experience for me if the alternative text was right because then I could engage right away and leave comments about what I love from those albums rather than spending time to figure out what the albums are."

Emails that are more images than text: All too often Joe finds emails that arrive with enticing subject lines like "Take 40% off." He opens the email to find a bunch of graphics without meaningful alternative text or no alternative text at all, and images that might be a link but that aren't labeled as to what the link's function is.

"I don't know if I need a coupon code. I don't know if I need to click on a link. Initially it sounds good, and I'll open the email to find out what it's about, but then I'm not able to engage and I don't want to put in the work to figure it out."

Accessibility is about providing equivalent content so anyone can engage, get the information they need, and make purchases. "When content is done well, you could sit a sighted person alongside a good user of a screen reader and they could probably get to the information, or to the product and purchase it, in a pretty similar time. It doesn't take that long."

Karla Hailer

Jeff met Karla through an online author community they belong to. She's a former journalist and is currently a teacher and multifaceted creative as she writes fiction, nonfiction, and poetry, and also quilts and paints.

Jeff shared early versions of possible covers for this book to the community, and one of Karla's comments caught our attention: "There's way too much stuff for my ADHD (attention deficit hyperactivity disorder) brain to parse… As it is, that's the type of book I would pass over." (You can find the cover Karla's commenting on at ContentForEveryone.info/book/early-cover.)

"They always say don't judge a book by a cover, yet we all do," Karla says. "There were all those moving parts, and a lot of the images were repeated. It was so busy and so loud in my mind."

That loudness would have had Karla skipping this book if she'd seen the cover on a retailer site. While this book isn't about book cover design, it illustrates the issues some people have when interacting with websites, social media, or emails.

Karla shared with us that her official ADHD diagnosis came when she was in her late 40s, but that she'd been developing tips and tricks to manage it for years before. For her it's about doing things to stay organized, including a color-coding system, taking notes using the sketchnoting method so that visuals are included, and creating to-do lists that work for her.

What affects Karla's experience on the web?

Just like she described with our book cover concept, if there are too many things going on in an image, or too many elements on a page, or something that's pulling focus on a page, Karla is likely to move on from it.

Her number one piece of advice: "It goes back to keep it simple, stupid. I don't need things fancied up and dressed up. Speak to me plainly and I'm okay. I feel like tricks treat you' like you're not intelligent. If you can't make your point without all sorts of flash and sizzle, then what's your point."

Karla needs more focus, so too many elements in an image, or not knowing where to look, or pop-ups randomly displaying and vying for attention are all things that will cause her to leave a site. "The more stuff that keeps trying to get my attention, the more overwhelming it becomes," she says.

Karla and her family also highlight what we mentioned at the start of this section: every person is unique. Within her family, Karla's children, her brothers, her father, and her nephews all have ADHD, and it's different for each of them. While Karla, for example, won't engage with TikTok because there's too much going on, one of her sons loves the format and making videos for it. In another case, one of her children can spend hours with video games whereas she and another of her sons don't like them. "It's different for each person, and people forget that."

That's a very important concept to reemphasize—it's impossible to generalize disabilities. Every person's situation is unique. When you follow the guidance we provide in this book, however, you will help everyone feel included when they engage with your content.

E.M. Lindsey

E.M. is an author and they have progressive hearing loss that started several years ago with tinnitus and has progressed from there. Even with their hearing aids and in a place with little background noise, they generally pick up only 30 to 40 percent of what's being said around them.

"I'm very, very good at reading the room. If I'm in a situation like a large gathering or in a noisy restaurant, I do a lot of nodding and smiling and just trying to pick up context clues about what's going on because everything can be like white noise all blending together."

For any audio and video on the internet, E.M. relies on captions or transcripts. While automated captions are becoming more widely available, E.M. is quick to state, "they are never great."

Regardless of the type of captions available, they always have them on because the captions along with the hearing aids help ensure they get as much information as possible.

The lack of captions in some cases means that E.M. has had to miss out on webinars and online classes on writing craft, marketing, and online ads because the creators did not include captions for the live sessions or the replays.

"I've spent a lot of money on some conferences that I couldn't access. There's a lot of marketing tools that people use, and those have accompanying videos with them to teach you how to do things like Amazon ads or Facebook ads, but they're not accessible."

Sometimes, the information is important enough to E.M. that they'll do the extra effort of watching multiple times to make sure they understand all the content. That, however, comes with a time cost and often is exhausting because of the cognitive drain of trying to process the difficult-to-hear audio information.

"I call it hearing fatigue, where my brain gets really tired of trying to understand. There comes a point where I just give up. It's the most frustrating with the marketing courses. I feel like I'm losing out on important information that other authors have easy access to."

The fatigue is part of the "disability tax," meaning the extra expense and frustration caused by certain things related to living with a disability. People who are disabled require technology or other items—whether it's hearing aids like E.M., a screen reader for someone who is blind, a wheelchair for a person who cannot walk, or other required things—that often cost money that is not always covered by insurance. Then there's the frustration caused by barriers, such as poor captions or no captions, that must also be dealt with.

As with the other people we talked to, E.M. hopes that education about accessible content will help increase its availability. When E.M. points out missing captions to course creators, the response is often, "I didn't even think about that."

"I've grown up around the disabled community," E.M. says. "I didn't realize how little most people knew until I stepped away from home. Then I was like, 'Okay, people aren't being deliberately ignorant. They just really don't know.'"

Heather Neff

Heather is the founder and CEO of Equivalent Design, but before that she was an artist with a Bachelor of Arts degree in painting and illustration. She's also got a background in web development and graphic design.

Heather credits the vision, cognitive, and motor disabilities that she developed later in life for making her a better designer as she became passionate about making accessible graphics and experiences for people.

Heather often encounters multiple barriers when

accessing web content. First and foremost, because of her vision impairment, she uses dark mode.

"I'll actually leave your website if it's a bright website," she says. "I need to either force your website into dark mode using an extension or use a custom contrast theme on my PC."

There are times neither of those options works well, so Heather may need to lower the contrast and brightness down on her monitor even more. This is particularly true on social media sites where some sites don't offer a dark theme, which means there's no dark mode availability even if dark mode is chosen on the device.

Color contrast between the text color and the background as well as the font style used can also present barriers to readability. In these cases, Heather might force dark mode through a plug-in or other methods she has available.

"I would love for every content creator to add a dark theme to their site," Heather says. "This is something that would change my life dramatically and reduce a lot of eyestrain and pain, and it would help millions of low vision and blind users as well."

You might be asking yourself why a blind user would benefit from dark mode. Some people who are legally blind have very limited sight. In some of these cases, the light from a bright screen can cause pain, so dark mode is helpful. This is why people who are blind might wear sunglasses as well, to protect their eyes from bright surroundings.

In terms of adding a dark theme to your website, that's not something you should tackle on your own unless you're also an experienced designer or developer, because getting it right is complex. If you have the opportunity to work with one on your site, however, you can discuss adding a dark theme with them.

Font size issues also crop up with marketing emails and websites that don't use a mobile-friendly design, which means the message text ends up too tiny to read. Using a mobile-friendly template is easy and they are readily available through email providers. "Making someone flip the phone horizontal and zoom in is unacceptable behavior at this time," she says.

With her motor disabilities, Heather is in physical pain if she uses her arms. This means she uses the keyboard and mouse sparingly, so she relies on voice control. However, if the site isn't developed correctly, she may not be able to use voice control to navigate, fill out forms, and perform other key tasks.

We don't expect you to be able to correct issues with voice control on your own, but it is important to be aware that members of your audience may navigate that way. This is another area where if you're working with a professional developer on your site, it is something to discuss with them.

Heather has some advice for content creators:

Colors: Make sure you're thinking about color-blind users and not relying on only color to convey meaning.

Fonts: Don't use text that's too small to be read. This can be a particular problem on social media and especially mobile devices when images that have text are used. The text in the image is often too small and can't be zoomed, making it impossible to read, and even if it can be zoomed, the text might get distorted and still be unreadable.

Language: Be aware of ableist language, such as "See information on the right." A nonsighted user won't be navigating the site visually or using direction like "on the right." Instead, use something like, "More information is available in the Practical Guide." Then visitors can search for the section title.

Focus: As much as possible, keep the number of calls to action on a page to a minimum to help your visitors stay focused on what you want them to do next. That will also result in less of a cognitive load on your audience, which means less fatigue.

Heather's hope for the future is that everyone gains an understanding of not just digital accessibility but inclusivity overall because it affects so many people and likely will affect everyone to some extent as they get older.

THE WEB CONTENT
ACCESSIBILITY GUIDELINES
AND WHAT THEY MEAN
TO YOU

BEFORE WE GET into what you can do, we want to give you some history and understanding of the bigger picture around website accessibility, of which content accessibility plays a part. Our intention is to keep the focus of this book narrow so you know the actions you can take, but understanding some of the broader concepts can be helpful too.

In this section we go beyond content. If you are a web developer or if you're working with one on your site, you'll find that there are more things to consider to make your site accessible.

For the nontechnical, we provide this detail so you'll have a broader understanding of why this is important and how it connects to the actions you can take that we'll detail in the "Practical Guide to Improving Your Content's Accessibility" section.

The History

Since 2000 the Web Content Accessibility Guidelines (WCAG) have been the primary reference for anyone working to understand what's needed to make a website accessible.[1] The WCAG were developed by the World Wide Web Consortium (W3C), the same organization that sets the standards for the web, including things like HTML and XML.

The Guidelines have been updated a few times over the past two decades—and we know there'll be further updates. However, the fundamentals that detail what's needed to make sure websites and other digital properties are accessible for everyone haven't changed.

The Guidelines' structure is simple:

Principles: There are four overarching principles. The principles contain one or more guidelines that detail what needs to be done to meet the principle.

Guidelines: There are 13 guidelines and they are divided into one or more success criteria that give the specifics of how to meet the guideline.

Success criteria: There are 78 success criteria, which provide the testable details to make an accessible website.

Levels: The success criteria divide into three levels:

- Level A: Baseline to ensure a website is accessible.
- Level AA: Extends accessibility to cover more scenarios.
- Level AAA: Excellence in accessibility.

Principles & Guidelines

As we write this book, WCAG 2.1 Level AA are the most referenced and accepted guidelines around the world. It's expected that in early 2023, WCAG 2.2 will be released. At this time, the update does not contain any items that we would cover in this book. You can check ContentForEveryone.info/book/wcag-updates to find any updates we might have.

Let's review the basics of how the principles and guidelines fit together so you understand the types of things that can be a roadblock to someone navigating your site and interacting with your content.

Principle 1: Perceivable

All content must be presented to users in ways they can perceive. In other words, the content shouldn't be available in just one way. It should be able to be read visually, via audio using a screen reader, and in a tactile fashion with a braille monitor.

Perceivable Guidelines

Text alternatives: For anything that isn't text, such as an image, you need to provide a meaningful text alternative. This text is needed for anyone who can't see the image or who may not process visual information as well as they might in another format. As a content creator, you have a lot of control over how this type of content is handled.

Time-based media (better known as audio, video, and multimedia): As with images, you need to provide alternative ways for users to understand the spoken words and other sounds in an audio program.

This can be done as a transcript, ideal for media like podcasts, or closed captions, which should be added to all videos with a soundtrack. Audio description of what's happening in a video also falls under this guideline. If you create multimedia of any kind, this is an important area for you.

Adaptable: Content creators need to think about areas of this guideline as it relates to making sure content is well organized and presented logically and meaningfully. This includes the proper use of headings and page titles.

Distinguishable: This guideline primarily deals with making sure elements in the foreground can be distinguished from the background. Examples of items to be aware of include how color is used and avoiding using images that have text in them.

Principle 2: Operable

Your site's controls, such as buttons, links, and form fields, must be operable and cannot require an operation the user can't perform. While this guideline is more technical, there are elements that a content creator can manage.

Operable Guidelines

Keyboard accessible: For users who cannot use a mouse or tap on a screen, it's important that they can use a keyboard to navigate.

While this isn't something you alone can easily change, you need to understand how your site works. This might be an area where you'd consider getting a new template or hiring an expert to help if keyboard navigation is not working correctly.

Enough time: Some users need more time to complete tasks or read content. This guideline is something you'll need to consider if you have anything on your site that changes or updates based on time, or if visitors have a set time in which to complete an activity.

Seizures: No one wants to cause seizures, but it's possible that you can if you're creating animated graphics or videos that have fast-pulsing red, white, and yellow colors.

Navigable: Your content needs to include ways for users to understand where they are, what content is available, and where they'll go if they follow a link. Good use of page titles, headings, and link text is key.

Input modalities: This guideline deals with how users interact, particularly on mobile devices and tablets, when tapping on the screen and performing swiping gestures. If you tackle this guideline at all, it would likely be when working with a skilled developer.

Principle 3: Understandable

As you'd expect, your audience should be able to understand your content and the website interface. These guidelines have the fundamental information to help you achieve this.

Understandable Guidelines

Readable: This one probably seems obvious, but there are steps you can take to ensure your content is easily read by anyone regardless of how they are reading.

Predictable: Making sure that your site and its individual pages behave in an expected and predictable way is key to a good experience for everyone. For example, you wouldn't want a completely different navigation header on every page of your site—it would be confusing.

Input assistance: This guideline speaks to the need for users to have a clear understanding about any information they may be required to enter in forms so they can avoid mistakes. Some of this guideline is more technical, but there are a few points that you'll want to make sure you're managing.

Principle 4: Robust

This is the most technical of the principles. It states that the site must be robust enough that it can be interpreted reliably by web browsers and assistive technology. Unless you're a skilled web developer or you have one working for you, there's not much you'll be able to manage. For completeness, however, it's worth knowing this principle.

Robust Guideline

Compatible: This is all about the compatibility with browsers and other technologies. If you're a web developer, you should do the necessary training around being able to manage this guideline.

WHAT CAN YOU DO?

Can I Find and Fix Accessibility Issues?

Yes, you can!

A primary principle to work by is "progress over perfection." This is the mantra of many who work on website accessibility. It can be overwhelming if you try to understand and work on everything at once.

Making progress—correcting areas of your website, improving how you manage your emails and social media posts, and changing how you approach any new content you create—makes a difference for your audience.

In particular "progress over perfection" is even more important for you since we don't expect you to be technical.

We imagine you're building your website with WordPress, Wix, or a similar platform. If you're sending newsletters, you're using something like MailChimp, MailerLite, ConvertKit, or something similar where you enter your text, images, and links using a provided template and then send it off. When you're working with images, you might use a program like Photoshop or online tools like Canva.

Our focus is helping you correct what you can and create

new content that is accessible in the simplest way possible. You'll need to spend some time reviewing your site based on what we cover in the "Practical Guide" section and then fixing issues that you find. You'll also want to consider our guidance for future content no matter where you're posting it.

Major Platforms and Their Accessibility Commitment

Every company approaches accessibility differently. Luckily, most of the website builders and email platform providers take it seriously. To understand the overall accessibility of the tools that you're using, you can easily research those online by simply doing a search for the platform name of your choice and the term "accessibility," such as "Wix accessibility."

Here are some examples we found:

Wix: The website has both "web accessibility" and "accessibility statement" in the footer at wix.com. "Web accessibility" details what someone using the Wix platform can do to make their site accessible. The "accessibility statement" offers details about the accessibility of the wix.com website itself.

WordPress: There are no links to accessibility information directly in the site footer at WordPress.org but it does include details as part of the "About" section.

MailChimp: There is an "accessibility" link in its footer at MailChimp.com, which links to accessibility information from their parent company, Intuit. If you do a web search for "MailChimp accessibility," you find links to articles in its "help" section about creating accessible newsletters.

Of course, if you're paying any platform to use their service, you can also directly ask them what their policies are for accessibility, what they do to ensure the accessibility of the platform, and the tools they make available to you to create accessible content.

Accessibility is not only for the final product (such as a website or email) but also for the interface you use to create it. Something to look for in a platform's information is that it not only conforms to the Web Content Accessibility Guidelines but also to the Authoring Tool Accessibility Guidelines (ATAG). The ATAG states that the platform itself is accessible (such as the interface to create a newsletter) and that authors can create accessible products (such as the finished newsletter).

We know changing platforms is time consuming and we're not saying it's something you must do. Understanding what each platform offers, however, can help inform any changes you might make in the future.

Also, keep in mind that even if the platform's commitment to accessibility isn't well documented or if the platform has accessibility gaps, you can still do the things we outline in the "Practical Guide" section to improve the content you're putting on whatever platform you're using.

What About Themes and Plug-ins?

Much like the platforms themselves, ideally the themes and plug-ins should also have accessibility information available. When you're searching for themes, WordPress in particular has a filter you can use to indicate you want one that's "Accessibility Ready." These templates have been reviewed by members of the WordPress community to ensure they meet basic standards.

One important note on themes: A theme might be accessible the first time you install it, and it might cover several accessibility requirements. However, you'll need to make sure it stays that way and to address other aspects of accessibility based on the content you add. For example, if you use colors that don't have good color contrast, then the theme's accessibility is lessened.

It's great to start with an accessible theme, but you'll need to do your part to keep it that way.

For both themes and plug-ins, you'll need to do your homework and review the documentation to understand if it includes details on accessibility. Sadly, in our experience, at this point many do not.

In the "Practical Guide" section, we mention ways that you can test key aspects of accessibility, and we'd recommend you do this for any theme or plug-in so you can understand the accessibility of what you're using.

Lastly, if you're paying for a custom theme or template, make sure to ask about accessibility if the details aren't already provided. If you're paying, you should absolutely get a product that's accessible so that you're providing a good experience to your entire audience.

Working with Developers and Designers

Sometimes you may work with graphic designers and website developers. Maybe you're creating new branding or launching a new project that needs a new website. Perhaps you're redesigning your website.

When you're doing something new, it's a perfect opportunity to make sure you're working with people who can deliver accessible graphic designs and websites.

Here are a couple of simple questions to ask:

Do you design and/or develop to meet the Web Content Accessibility Guidelines? If they say no or that they don't know what that means, try to find someone else to do the work you need. If they say yes, that's great and hopefully they are being honest about their skills (sadly, we've encountered instances where that's not always the case).

How do you test for accessibility? If they say that they only scan for issues, you'll know they are not doing enough for the reasons we'll explain in the "What Can You Find with an Accessibility Scan" section. The answer you want to get is that they use both a scan *and* manual checks that include keyboard navigation and other assistive technologies, such as a screen reader.

Automatic Fixes: If It Sounds Too Good to Be True, It Is

You may find various plug-ins, widgets, and overlays that claim to fix accessibility issues automatically. Some of these are free, and others have monthly fees. Please don't use these to make your site accessible. At this time, they can cause more problems than they solve.

There are two major reasons these products can't magically make a website accessible. First, only a small fraction of accessibility issues can be detected by an automated test. Even if you use a plug-in or widget, you're not solving for all the potential problems.

More importantly, tools that claim to manage accessibility automatically have a history of interfering with assistive technology and causing more issues than they solve for site visitors. As you can imagine, interference is not a good experience for the user.

In summary, please avoid adding these to your website and don't let anyone talk you into them as a fast way to fix content accessibility.

Tell Your Visitors Accessibility Matters to You

Alongside any cookie and privacy policies you may have on your site, we'd recommend including an accessibility statement as well. The statement doesn't have to be long, but it should contain three key things:

- State that accessibility is important to you.
- State that you're doing what you can to ensure your site is accessible.
- Give users a way to contact you if they have any issues.

You can review examples of accessibility statements that we use in the footer of ContentForEveryone.info and that Jeff uses at BigGayFictionPodcast.com and JeffAdamsWrites.com. You can even use those as a template to create your own.

Of course, if you're going to add the statement, please make sure you're taking the needed steps to make your site accessible. Otherwise, the words are meaningless. You'll also need to regularly check the associated contact mailbox and be ready to provide assistance to everyone asking.

This is another good moment to remind you that we are not attorneys and are not providing legal advice regarding what information should be in the accessibility statement. We're simply providing guidance based on our expertise.

PRACTICAL GUIDE TO
IMPROVING YOUR
CONTENT'S ACCESSIBILITY

THE FOLLOWING 16 chapters explain common issues that arise with accessibility on websites, emails, and in social media posts.

As we mentioned earlier, we aren't covering everything about digital accessibility in this book since we expect that you aren't a developer. We want to discuss things you can find and fix with the platform that you use for your website and email marketing campaigns as well as when you're posting on the social channels that you use.

Let's get started.

Take a deep breath!

Maybe get a pen and paper so you can take notes about areas you want to review. In fact, you could download the *Content for Everyone* worksheet at ContentForEveryone.info/book/worksheet and use it.

Remember what we said previously about progress over perfection. As with most creative endeavors, it's not about attaining perfection. It's about making progress and putting your best possible work in front of your audience.

We're going to tell you a lot of things you can and should do to make your content accessible for everyone.

It is not necessary or even reasonable for you to do it all at once.

You don't have to stop what you're working on and do it right now.

These are things you can tackle page by page or issue by issue.

You could take in all this information and not fix any of your current content but use this knowledge to create accessible content going forward.

If you're doing something to make your content more accessible, you're doing the right thing.

About the Practical Guide

For each item, we'll summarize the issue and let you know how to find it and manage it correctly. You'll also find a section on what your next step should be, both to review current content and when you create something new. Lastly, we'll tell you who will benefit when you create content with accessibility in mind.

There will also be a cross-reference to the Web Content Accessibility Guidelines (WCAG) so you'll know which guidelines and success criteria are involved in case you want to get more detail, or if you're discussing these items with a web designer or developer.

1. IMAGES/NON-TEXT CONTENT

WORKING with images and other forms of non-text content, which include charts, graphs, infographics, audio and video, and anything else that is not simple text on the page, is fundamental to an accessible website.

Ensuring your visitors can understand and interact with all the content is important, and as a creative you're likely using a lot of non-text content.

On a basic level, each piece of non-text content must have a text alternative available for those who may not be able to visually perceive the content.

This may sound easy, and fundamentally it is, but there are many considerations to keep in mind because the context for the non-text content matters as you determine what alternative to provide.

Within this section we will not discuss audio and video. There are many considerations for that type of content, so it gets its own section, "Audio & Video."

Images

Images are used for many things, including but not limited to:

- Showing the items you're creating.
- Displaying what you're selling.
- Illustrating content you write.
- Providing visual interest.
- Creating the correct spacing (in those cases images will be invisible). There can also be invisible images for certain tracking pixels, such as Facebook and analytics.

You'll need to decide for each image the alternative text that should accompany it based on where it's displayed and the information it provides in the context of the rest of the content.

As you add images to your content, there should be a field for "alternative text" or "alt text." Most website and email platforms allow you to add alt text in this way, as do social media platforms. If you can't locate where to enter alternative text, check the platform's help documentation.

In addition, some platforms, such as WordPress, also have a checkbox or other method to indicate the image is decorative, which will confirm that the alternative text is deliberately left empty.

You can find some examples of these fields at ContentForEveryone.info/book/alternative-text-entry.

The platforms you use should automatically add an alt attribute to each image you're using. If you're working directly with the HTML on a page, you'll want to make sure you add an alt attribute and any needed text into the image tag. For example:

```
<img src="https://yoursite.com/imagename.jpg" alt="[alternative text goes here]">
```

And if you were going to leave the alt text empty because the image is decorative, the code would look like this with the alt attribute empty:

```
<img src="https://yoursite.com/imagename.jpg" alt="">
```

Creating meaningful alternative text for your images is crucial. *Meaningful* is the key word because the text needs to give users the details they need to understand what the image is if they can't see it. Don't make the common mistakes of allowing alternative text to be the image file name, only the word "image," or other nonsense that has nothing to do with the image and its meaning on the page.

One important tip on creating the meaningful text is don't start with "image of…" Screen readers and other assistive technology already announce "image." So if you began with "image of…" a screen reader would say "Image. Image of…" so it's best to avoid that.

Context Matters

For each image, you must consider the context it's presented in to determine what else needs to be added so any visitor who cannot visually perceive the image gets the complete story.

Here are two scenarios that call for a different handling of alternative text for images.

Scenario 1: If the image is next to the content that describes all the important information from the image, it can be considered decorative and the alt attribute left empty. Some examples:

An image of a book cover on an author's website page alongside the blurb of the book and links for where to purchase. Here the image could have no alternative text because the image is decorative to the page. The visitor doesn't need to know about the book cover because the important information for the book is the blurb and purchase details.

Optionally, you could make the alternative text be a short description of the book cover's imagery to offer more details about the story as it relates to the cover, but it wouldn't be required.

A piece of jewelry is shown next to details about the piece. The details include information like what it's made of, the colors, and what it looks like. If all the visual information is present in the on-page description, you don't need alternative text.

Some images, by their very nature, are decorative. For example, if you use any graphics to separate sections of a page or to add pure visual interest, these should have an empty alternative text.

Scenario 2: If the content adjacent to the image doesn't include all the details from the image, then the alternative text needs to include the rest of the details. Some examples:

An image of a book cover on a cover designer's website. If a cover image is on a designer's website as a cover available for purchase, it would need alternative text to describe the cover.

If someone came to a page of cover art with a heading of "Fantasy Covers," more information needs to be available about each cover to describe its appearance so that visitors who can't see the image can understand the artist's work.

On a page where a T-shirt is available for purchase. If the only text on page is the name of the design, such as "I Love Books," along with the fabric used and the sizes and colors available, more information is required in the alternative text about the design itself to inform a visitor's purchase decision. You could also add that information into the description on the page itself, as long as it's available somewhere for those who are blind and using assistive technologies to get the details.

A blog post with the title of "My Workspace" and images of a desk, bookshelves, and artwork on the walls. First, you should reconsider presenting an images-only post since getting all the details about the images into alt text might be too much. Instead, discuss each image with some text on the page so that you can split up the description between the alt text and the on-page content.

A good rule of thumb as you're considering alternative text and what's needed based on the other content on the page is to think about what information is missing for anyone who cannot see the image. If that information is key to understanding your message, either add to the page or to the alternative text. Make sure your visitors get complete, equal information by whatever means they choose to receive it.

Special Considerations

Linked images: If an image is a link, the alternative text must indicate where the link is going. Link destination is more important to provide than a description of the image.

Animated images: Animated GIFs are wildly popular, but they can be problematic because they can be an annoying distraction for some, not allowing them to focus on what they're trying to do. For others, they can possibly cause seizures, migraines, and vertigo.

If you're using animated GIFs, make sure they're necessary and make sure there's a way for users to stop them from constantly playing. Of course, make sure they have proper alt text as well for those who can't visually perceive them.

Images in carousels: If you're using a carousel, there are many elements of accessibility to consider (we'll talk more about them in "Auto Play Elements: Carousels, Videos, Animations"). For each image in a carousel, you must provide meaningful alternative text to describe it so anyone moving through the images can understand what the image is. We'd recommend this even if the image is decorative to ensure an equivalent carousel experience for all visitors.

Plus, consider that in most cases, images in a carousel will be links to somewhere else. Linked images, of course, must have meaningful alternative text that indicates where the link goes.

Charts: There can often be many ways to describe a chart that has many data points. Consider what you can state within the page content adjacent to the chart and what should be in alternative text. Make sure you provide all the data needed so everyone can understand the message of the chart.

Tests or quizzes: These can be tricky because you don't want to give away the answers in alternative text. For example, imagine a picture of fruit and a question asks how many apples are there? In the alternative text, you wouldn't want to state how many apples are present.

What you should do in instances like this is be as descriptive as possible without providing the test answers, such as "Various quantities of apples, oranges, and peaches." Visitors will understand from the page's context, including the test question, why you're not being specific.

Content providing a sensory experience: Sometimes a specific sensory experience is desired, such as listening to a symphony performance or viewing a painting. In those cases, provide alternative text or text on the page to describe as much as possible so that visitors are aware of the content's purpose.

CAPTCHA and questions to prove someone is human: You may have instances on your site where you're using CAPTCHA to help control spam in site comments, with email sign-ups, or other functions. Do your best to ensure these are accessible, such as a CAPTCHA module that includes an option to have the alphanumeric characters read out via audio.

Items like CAPTCHA are a good reason to have contact details in your accessibility statement so if a visitor has any trouble, they can get in touch with you to assist them if they can't move past a CAPTCHA check.

Notes About Email and Social Media

On email platforms, as you're adding images, you should find an option to add alternative text with the other image controls that are available.

Most social media platforms have a way for you to include alternative text for images:

Facebook: You'll find "edit alt text" as part of the options for editing an image.

Twitter: "Add description" or "+ALT" is part of the options available when you upload an image.

Instagram: When you're creating a post, you'll find the

place to add alt text under "Advanced Settings" > "Accessibility" > "Write Alt Text"

If you are using images on a platform that doesn't support alternative text, make sure to include details in the post itself. If you're not able to include the image details within the text seamlessly, you could add "Image description:" followed by the detail you would've placed in the alternative text.

And lastly, absolutely do not use auto-generated alternative text. It's often wrong about what's meaningful in the image, not well formatted, and might cause confusion rather than help.

You can check out some examples of poor auto-generated alternative text at ContentForEveryone.info/book/automatic. We're sure once you understand how bad this can be for your audience, you'll never let artificial intelligence do the job for you.

It's important to note that, as of this writing, Facebook and Instagram populate the alternative text field with auto-generated text. You'll want to make sure that you replace the alt text on those platforms with meaningful details. Leaving the text blank isn't an option, even if the image could be considered decorative.

One last note on social media: if you use any type of scheduler to make posts for you, make sure it has the fields available for you to add alt text as you're scheduling since some platforms, such as Twitter, won't let you make edits after the post is made.

Your Next Step

Review your current website content: Within the interface used to create posts and pages, you should be able to select images and be able to edit them. Within the edit screen, you should find the place to update/enter the alternative text.

You can also check this directly within the code of the post or page. If you go to the HTML view that's available within your post/page editor, you'll find the alt attribute and its contents as part of the "img" tag.

For Future Content

Website: For each image and non-text element you use, consider what its alternative text will be at the same time you're creating the content that it will be displayed with. Make sure you're following our guidance on writing meaningful alternative text as well as when to leave the alt text blank.

Emails: When you're creating new emails, make sure to fill out the alt text field (or leave it blank in case the image is decorative) as needed considering the content of the text adjacent to the image.

If you create a new newsletter by copying from a previous one and replacing content, don't forget to update the alt text fields as well so that you're not presenting text from a previous email.

Social media: As you create new posts, always make sure to add meaningful alternative text so that automated alt text won't be added by the platform.

Who Benefits?

Visually impaired: Anyone who has difficulty perceiving visual content can use their assistive technology to present the alternative text to them.

Cognitively impaired: Text alternatives can help people

who have difficulty understanding the meaning of photographs, drawings, charts, and other types of non-text information. These visitors may also use screen reader technology, even if they're also visually reviewing the page. The screen reader may allow them to understand the page better than if they were only taking in the information visually.

Everyone: If visitors have images turned off for any reason, the alternative text appears on screen to let users know what image is in that space.

Additionally, text alternatives support the ability to search for non-text content and to repurpose content in a variety of ways. Alternative text also helps your search engine optimization because the text is part of what search engines use to understand your site.

WCAG Reference

Guideline: Text Alternatives / Success Criterion: 1.1.1 Non-text Content

2. IMAGES OF TEXT

IMAGES OF TEXT are a special class of images. Despite their popularity for conveying information with visual interest, they are never fully accessible.

Anytime you're using an image of text, you must present all the text information in other ways to make sure everyone can access the content.

There are many reasons to avoid using images of text whenever possible.

The text in the image isn't available to assistive technologies, such as screen readers. Further, even if you add the text from the image into the alternative text, users who don't use assistive technology may have difficulty.

The text can be difficult for visitors with low vision or other visual impairments, such as color blindness, to read effectively. Cognitively disabled users may have trouble parsing the font used or separating the text from the visual background. In all instances, since the text is part of the image, users won't be able to adjust the font, size, or color for their needs.

If you must use images that have embedded text, there are

several things you can do to help site visitors perceive the information in the image.

Font selection: Make sure the text is in an easy-to-read font and size. Make the content readable for those who are viewing the image.

Color selection: The text needs to be in a color that stands out from the background. We'll talk more about that in the "Use of Color/Color Contrast" section.

Even with appropriate fonts and colors, the image's text should also be on the page alongside the image so it is easily available to all visitors regardless of how they're engaging with the content. The text can, of course, be reworded so it's not an exact duplication, but it should be an equivalent so the meaning is the same.

As you're taking the above steps, keep in mind the information we detailed in the "Images/Non-text Content" section, as all those rules also apply. You just have more to consider when text also appears in the image for how you'll make sure everyone who engages with your content gets the complete message.

Special Considerations

Sometimes using an image of text is acceptable, such as when it's part of the logo for your business.

It's also acceptable if an image of text is required. For example, if you're creating fonts, you would need to show an image of the font since it may not render correctly in a browser. The same is true for book covers, artwork, and designs that you're creating as part of your creative products.

Notes About Social Media

There's an abundance of images of text on social media. Everyone creating content must be thoughtful to ensure that everyone can perceive the messages. We've found messages that use images of text (and nothing else) for:

- Official information coming from all levels of government, such as emergency information.
- Notification of cancellation of or changes to events.
- Information of all types, from sales to event details to product reviews and just about anything else you can imagine.
- Screenshots of social media posts, which turn posts that may have been accessible in their original format into images of text.
- Memes, which of course are based on the idea of adding text to an image, often an animated GIF. (If you missed it, we discussed the problems with animated GIFs in the "Images/Non-text Content" section.)

When you're on social media sites, take a moment to observe the massive amount of content that might not be accessible to everyone.

While social media is a very visual medium, especially Instagram and TikTok, you must take care to ensure the messages are available to everyone—and even more so for posts that deliver vital information. This means the text that's in the image also needs to be part of the text of the post.

Your Next Step

Review your current website content: Review the images on your site. For the ones that have text in them, consider whether to replace them or to add additional text to the page so that the information in the image is available to everyone.

For Future Content

Website, emails, and social media: Of course, we'd prefer for everyone to stop using images with text embedded in them. However, we also know that's not always practical (case in point, Jeff often uses images of text for book and podcast promotion).

If you're using images of text, follow our guidance to make sure the text is easy to read, but also make sure the text is represented in the on-screen text content adjacent to the image so the content is available to everyone.

Remember, just having the content as alternative text doesn't make it perceivable by all users.

Who Benefits?

Visually impaired: People who may have trouble reading the image's text because of the font, size, and color used. In addition, users with visual tracking problems, who may have trouble reading the text with the line spacing and/or alignment used.

Of course, blind users who use a screen reader will be able to access the information if the alternative text has been properly set.

Cognitively impaired: People who have difficulties with

text comprehension, such as dyslexia, will receive the information when it is presented as part of the regular text on screen.

WCAG Reference
Guideline: Distinguishable / Success Criterion: 1.4.5 Images of Text

3. PAGE TITLES

THIS IS such a simple thing but one that sometimes is overlooked in favor of having only the site name as the title for every page.

Each page should have a unique title that clearly indicates the content of the page. How page titles are managed in your specific platform is determined in the settings area, but the simple rule of thumb is that you want the title of the page to be first, followed by a delimiter like a bullet or pipe symbol, the step of the multipage process (if applicable), followed by another delimiter, and then the name of the site. The exception to that is the home page, which should be the name of the site and perhaps some details about the site itself.

Here are a few examples from JeffAdamsWrites.com:

Home page: Jeff Adams Writes | Gay Romances and LGBTQ+ Young Adult Fiction

Page with all of Jeff's books: Books by Jeff Adams | Jeff Adams Writes

Page featuring a specific genre: Young Adult Books by Jeff Adams | Jeff Adams Writes

Page for a specific book: Tracker Hacker (Codename: Winger 1) by Jeff Adams | Jeff Adams Writes

Another example is if you have any sort of multistep process on your site, such as going through checkout to make a purchase. You should indicate which step the visitor is on, such as: Checkout Step 1: Shipping Information | Jeff Adams Writes.

These titles make it clear what someone will find on the page.

Your Next Step

Review your current website content: Review the pages on your website and observe what appears in the browser's title tab. If they're already unique and meaningful, you're good to go.

In general, website platforms make the page title the same as the title you give a post or page. However, sometimes your site's overall admin settings may dictate what's used for the page titles. If necessary, consult your platform's help documentation for how to set page titles.

For Future Content

Website: Always create new pages and posts with unique page titles. Once you review how your site creates them by default, this should be easy to do.

Emails and social media: This is not applicable for emails and social media posts. It is worth noting, however, that for emails the subject of the email will become the page title if the email is viewed in the browser. Making the subject the page title is handled by the email platform and not something you have to consider separately.

Who Benefits?

Everyone: Ability to quickly and easily identify if the page is relevant to the content they want.

Visually impaired: Those using screen readers or other assistive technologies will know as they go from page to page, or if they have multiple pages open, what page they are currently on.

Cognitively impaired: Identifying page content by its title can be important for those with attention deficit, short-term memory loss, and other impairments.

Motor impaired: Those who might navigate the web with voice commands can speak the name of the page they want since unique page titles ensure that there is only one page with the title requested.

Your site overall also benefits from these rules since good page titling helps search engine optimization.

WCAG Reference
Guideline: Navigable / Success Criterion: 2.4.2 Page Titled

4. HEADINGS

THIS IS another item that is super easy to do right, but it's often not due to a lack of understanding of how to use headings.

Headings are designed to organize content on a page. In fact, if you've got subheads on pages that are simply bold text, these should likely be headings.

It's important to make that change too. According to a 2019 WebAIM (Web Accessibility in Mind) survey of screen reader users, more than 65% review a page's headings to understand and navigate content.[1]

In our interview with Joe DiNero in the "Accessing Content on the Web" section, he mentioned his frustration when headings are not available. If you're not using headings right or not using them at all, you're not helping site visitors get to the content they want quickly and efficiently.

In your website platform and sometimes in email platforms as well, within the window where you enter content, there's usually a menu to select style alongside the buttons to select bold, italics, and other formatting. Within that are

Headings 1 through 6 (or sometimes listed as H1 through H6).

Too often these Heading levels are used for visual impact because of the font size they're assigned or other visual style that is applied. However, that's a misuse that can cause confusion and frustration. A good way to consider headings is like an outline for the content on the page.

We'll use Jeff's book page at JeffAdamsWrites.com as a simple example.

Heading 1: This is the title of the page (in this case "Books"), which appears at the top of the page as well as in the browser tab for the page title.

Most WordPress and Wix themes, for example, set this automatically since Heading 1, in most cases, should be the same as the page title. There should only be one Heading 1 per page.

Heading 2: There are several Heading 2 subheads to meaningfully divide up the books into categories, such as "Romances" and "Young Adult."

Heading 3: Several Heading 3 subheads are in place to divide up some categories further, such as "Novels & Novellas" and "Short Stories."

In the above example, there are only three heading levels needed to organize content.

Some pages require more, however. An example is a *Big Gay Fiction Podcast* episode page. Here's the typical heading layout for an episode:

Heading 1: Title of the episode.

Heading 2: There are usually two Heading 2 subheads per episode, one for the show notes section and one for the episode transcript. This allows visitors to quickly find these main sections.

Heading 3: Within the transcript, Heading 3 designates

episode sections, such as "Intro," "Book Reviews," "Interview," and "Wrap-Up."

Heading 4: These are used when there's a need to further divide information. For example, a Heading 3, such as "Book Reviews," can have several Heading 4 subheads used to identify a specific book.

You'll want to use headings in order, with proper nesting. For example, using the above example from the podcast:

Heading 1: Title of Episode
Heading 2: Show Notes
Heading 2: Episode Transcript
Heading 3: Intro
Heading 3: Book Reviews
Heading 4: Book Title One
Heading 4: Book Title Two
Heading 3: Interview with Author
Heading 3: Wrap-Up

This order is correct because everything is nested. It's okay that there is not a Heading 3 under "Show Notes" because that content didn't need further subdividing. It's also correct to have multiple Heading 4s under a single Heading 3.

Here's an example, however, that violates the WCAG (and causes accessibility issues) because a heading level is skipped.

Heading 1: Title of Episode
Heading 2: Show Notes
Heading 2: Transcript
Heading 3: Intro
Heading 2: Book Reviews
Heading 4: Book Title One

Heading 4: Book Title Two
Heading 3: Interview with Author
Heading 3: Wrap-Up

"Heading 2: Book Reviews" is wrong because it moves "Book Reviews" on the same level of hierarchy as "Transcript" when actually "Book Reviews" is a section of the transcript. Also, there are Heading 4 subheads coming after a Heading 2. Heading 4 should only follow Heading 3. The ordering is important so site visitors understand the organization of the content.

If you'd like to see these examples along with another on an actual page, go to ContentForEveryone.info/book/headings.

We mentioned many people use headings solely for styling purposes, for example to control the size of subheads. If you're doing that, please stop and ensure you're only using them to organize content.

We encourage you to explore your platform and theme so you understand how to adjust text size when needed so that you're using headings for their intended purpose.

Your theme should also have controls for you to set the text size for headings so that they make sense visually as part of content organization.

Note About Email

Depending on your email platform and the email template you're using, you may not have a lot of choices on how headings are set. For example, we've found some templates where the content blocks all assign Heading 1 for the headline of the block, and there's no way for the user to change that.

Of course, you can only work within the parameters of the

platform, but understanding good heading structure and what your platform permits will allow you to organize your emails in the best way possible, no matter how your recipients are engaging with the content.

Your Next Step

Review your current website content: You probably have a few page types on your site, such as the home page, blog pages, product pages, and maybe some others. Review a sample or two of each type and determine if you're using the heading levels correctly, which you can easily check by going into the editor for each page and placing your cursor on the subheads.

If you're using a heading, the selector in the editor should show you what it is. If you're working with the HTML code, review what's in the "h" tags, like "<h1>".

If you find you're not using headings correctly, you can decide if you're going to fix them or only create future pages correctly.

We would suggest that even if you're not going to change all your pages, you update your home page and highest trafficked pages to improve the experience on them.

For Future Content

Website: As you create new text content, consider as you write how you'll use headings. Thinking about that from the start allows you to make sure the organization of the content is logical and that you'll structure headings correctly.

Emails: Your email template likely has preset headings that you cannot change (at least, that's been our experience), so there's nothing you can do here unless you've got control over all the HTML of your template. If that's the case, you can adjust and/or create the headings with the "h" tags.

Social media: This is not applicable for social media posts.

Who Benefits?

Everyone: Organizing content meaningfully helps everyone determine what sections contain the information that's desired and allows the page to be scanned quickly regardless of if someone is reviewing the page visually or using assistive technologies.

Visually impaired: Those who use screen readers are helped when you ensure headings are meaningful, as it allows them to understand content organization. Assistive technology users often prefer to access the list of headings to quickly navigate to the content they want.

Also, visitors with low vision who can see only a few words at a time are helped by having short, meaningful headings.

Cognitively impaired: Descriptive headings are useful for visitors who may read more slowly as well as for those with limited short-term memory. For these visitors, headings make it possible to predict what each section contains.

WCAG References
Guideline: Adaptable / Success Criterion: 1.3.1 Info and Relationships
Guideline: Navigable / Success Criterion: 2.4.6 Headings and Labels

5. USE OF COLOR/COLOR CONTRAST

HOW COLOR IS USED IS a large part of the visual design of a website and usually carries over to email design. There are areas of color usage that need attention where accessibility is concerned.

- Using color as the only designation that something is important and/or actionable.
- Maintaining proper color contrast for text and non-text content to ensure it stands out from the color(s) in the background.

Color as a Designation

It's not wrong to use color as a designation, but it cannot be the only way you call attention to an item. This occurs in two common areas:

Links: For links, the fix is simple. Besides whatever color your links are, add an underline. At some point, having an underline for links fell out of favor, but it's the perfect way to ensure links are perceivable to everyone visually interacting with the screen.

To indicate important information: If you're using color to highlight the importance of something or an item that needs attention, you need to make sure you're identifying that content in a way that doesn't rely only on color.

Here are three examples:

Alert messages: If you've got an important message in red, add text preceding it, such as "important," "alert," or something similar, to call it out. You could add an image or icon, such as a stop sign or exclamation point, to draw attention in a way that doesn't rely on the color. Of course, any image or icon you add must meet the color contrast requirements for non-text content.

Error messaging: If you've got forms, such as email sign-ups, comments, or a shopping cart checkout, take a moment to make sure, if those are using color as a designation, that they're doing it in an accessible way.

An error message at the top of the page that reads "Fields marked in red have errors" is not accessible because there are users who can't perceive the color. "Please fix the errors in the email and phone number fields" is accessible, and those fields can still be highlighted in red accompanied by the specific error message.

We understand that you're likely not able to fix forms that have this kind of error, but you can work to replace them with forms that are accessible or work with a developer who can make changes. Your site visitors will appreciate that you took this step.

Color coding: If you're creating something with a legend, such as a schedule or chart that uses color to designate categories or other organizational aspects, consider that if color is all you're designating with, the entire chart could look gray to some people.

To solve this, you could add a pattern in addition to the color so there's additional distinction. Of course, you'd still need other alternative text since this would also be classified as non-text content, so you'd have to follow the guidance in the "Images/Non-text Content" section as well.

Color Contrast

You've probably been to websites that have color combinations that make the content difficult to read even if your vision is perfect. The rules for color contrast are in place to ensure that text is readable for the widest number of visitors.

Simply put, color contrast is the difference in perceived brightness between two colors. For standard sized text, the contrast must be at least 4.5:1. Large text, over 18 point or 14 point bold, must have a contrast of at least 3:1.

For fonts that are thin or are unusual, the ratio may need to be higher to ensure readability.

In the section on "Images of Text," we mentioned that if you're going to have text embedded in an image, you need to ensure it meets color contrast rules. It can be a challenge, with the text possibly going across many colors, depending on the image.

Following color contrast rules is necessary to help people who are visually engaging with the image to be able to read the text.

Along with text against a background, you need to also consider the color contrast of other elements such as buttons, form fields, and focus indicators. This would extend to the example we gave earlier about color coding. Those colors would also need to have proper contrast against the page background and the other colors that are used.

Site visitors need to be able to clearly perceive all the elements on the page, so make sure the non-text elements have a contrast ratio of at least 3:1 when compared to the background color.

Figuring out color contrast is easy. The color contrast checker provided by WebAIM at webaim.org/resources/contrastchecker/ is simple to use.

- Get the hex codes for the colors you want to test. You should be able to access those codes from any number of design tools you use.
- Enter the hex codes for the foreground and background colors into the checker.
- The result instantly displays, and you'll know if the color combination passes or fails for regular and large text.
- The checker also has controls so you can increase and decrease the brightness to find a color combination that meets the proper contrast ratio.

Your Next Step

Review your current website and email content: For color contrast: Most likely your site and email templates have a set color palette that is managed in the admin settings.

You can use the contrast checker we recommended to check that those colors pass. If the colors don't pass, you can change them across the entire template through the settings.

For use of color: Review how you're using color on your site and email templates by checking the key page types— home page, blog page, product page, other general content pages, and the email template—and make note of anything you should update.

For Future Content

Website and emails: As you're using colors, make sure the color combinations always pass the color contrast checker so everyone can read clearly. Of course, you'll also want to make sure that color isn't being used as the only way that something is distinguished.

The majority of this will be handled by the settings in your templates, which hopefully you've corrected as part of your review so that you won't have to think about this unless you're doing new color customizations.

Social media: For general text posts, there's not much you can adjust for colors on the platforms. However, when you're creating things like Instagram Stories or TikTok posts, be aware of the color combinations you're using for text over backgrounds and make sure the contrast is as high as possible so the text is accessible.

Who Benefits?

Everyone: Clear, sharp text makes the reading experience better for everyone.

Visually impaired: Site visitors with partial sight as well as some older users often experience limited color vision, so proper color contrast helps ensure they can interact with and understand your content.

Visitors with color blindness or who have problems distinguishing between colors can perceive information that is conveyed by color when it is also available in other visual ways, such as underlining links or providing other visual cues. Proper color contrast also increases the chance they'll be able to see the text.

Anyone using text-only, limited color, or monochrome displays may not be able to understand any meanings that are conveyed through color alone.

People using any type of screen reader, where color would not be identifiable, can be made aware of important information when it's conveyed in an alternative manner.

Cognitively impaired: From a color contrast perspective, having the correct color contrast makes the reading experience better and easier since these visitors might already be putting in more effort to read your site. You don't want to add to the effort by having poor color contrast.

Also, where the use of color is concerned, site visitors might not understand the meaning behind the color, so any important messages you're conveying should not be through color alone.

WCAG References

Guideline: Distinguishable / Success Criterion: 1.4.1 Use of Color
Guideline: Distinguishable / Success Criterion: 1.4.3 Color Contrast (Minimum)
Guideline: Distinguishable / Success Criterion: 1.4.11 Non-text Contrast

6. LINK TEXT

CLEARLY STATING where links lead to is easy but so often overlooked in favor of simply linking the words "click here" or "read more." Another common problem is to have many links on a page that all have the same text, such as "buy now" and the aforementioned "click here" and "read more."

Consider as well that for some users, the terms "click" and "here" will be ambiguous because they may not use a device that relies on clicks to follow a link or perhaps they cannot see where "here" is.

Further, for anyone navigating via voice control, a bunch of links that are all labeled the same will prevent them from being able to speak the name of the link they wish to visit.

Then there's the image that's a link, which might not clearly indicate where the link will go. Perhaps there's text in that image that does state where the link goes, but as mentioned in the "Images of Text" section, not everyone will be able to perceive that text.

When you're creating a link within WordPress, Wix, many email interfaces, and other platforms, there are fields for the "Link Text," which is what appears on the page if you're making a text link. This is the essential information about the link and where it will take the user. "Link Text" is available to assistive technology users in every scenario. Also, there is often the field for "Title," and this is a field you can use for bonus detail. "Title" is for bonus detail only because it is not always available to users.

Here are some examples on how to create meaningful text links by adding more to the text that's being linked:

This is an example of a link that could be improved:
For more information about my book, <u>click here</u>.

Instead, link the entire sentence and make it clear what book you're referencing:
<u>For more information about *Content for Everyone*, click here.</u>

Even better would be to eliminate the "click here:"
<u>Get more information about *Content for Everyone*.</u>

Or you could be more specific by indicating where the information is going to be found:
<u>Get more information about *Content for Everyone* on MyBookstore.com.</u>

Remember, if you're linking an image, the alternative text must have the information about the link. For example, if you're displaying the logos for all the places you can get a podcast and those logos are links, the alt text for the logos should state the name of the podcast and the service you're linking to. Example: "Listen to Big Gay Fiction Podcast at Spotify."

If for any reason the link text isn't enough for the visitor to understand where the link is going, or if you can't avoid multiple links with the same text, you can also use the "Title" field to provide that bonus information.

This is something that Jeff uses on *Big Gay Fiction Podcast* since every episode has a link for podcast providers. As part of the link for "Apple Podcasts," for example, he'll add "Title" information so it's clear which episode the link is for, such as "Get episode 391 on Apple Podcasts."

One last note about links: Our recommendation is not to have links open a new tab or window unless absolutely essential. This can be disorienting to people who are blind and use screen readers and some people with cognitive disabilities.

If you feel you must do this, make sure it's clear from the link text or by using the "Title" attribute that a new window will open so the user is prepared for it. You can review an example where we call out a new window opening at ContentForEveryone.info/book/headings. We felt the new window was necessary here since we commented on examples that were on another website.

While you want people to stay on your website and continue to engage with your content, have faith that people will use the back button, their browser history, or some other method when they are ready to return to your site.

Your Next Step

Review your current website content: Unless you know how you're managing links, this could be something you need to review on every page of the site. We'd recommend making sure your home page and the pages that are most important to your business have links that follow these best practices. But if you've got a lot of content, like a blog you've added hundreds of posts to over time, it probably isn't worth the time to fix all that content.

For Future Content

Website and emails: When writing new content, be deliberate with your link text so that your site's audience will know exactly what to expect when they activate it. It can be very tempting to fall back to "click here"-type links because they are easier to write into content, but your visitors will appreciate that you took the extra effort.

Social media: This isn't applicable for social media posts since how links are represented is controlled by the platforms.

Who Benefits?

Everyone: No matter how someone is reading your content, making it clear where links go improves the experience and allows everyone to find the information they need quickly.

Visually impaired: These users will be able to determine the purpose of a link by the link text as well as the contextual information around it. Assistive technologies present a list of links so information on the link purpose is easily available.

Motor impaired: Users can skip links they are not interested in, avoiding additional keystrokes to review linked content and the effort to return to the original page if that content wasn't what they wanted or expected.

Cognitively impaired: These people will not become disoriented by links that all have the same text or have little context about their destination.

WCAG Reference
Guideline: Navigable / Success Criterion: 2.4.4 Link Purpose (In Context)

7. LANGUAGE OF THE PAGE/PARTS OF THE PAGE

SETTING the language properly should be quite easy to accomplish. If you're using a platform like WordPress or Wix, you're asked to set the language for the site when you're setting it up. That becomes the default language for every page you create, and that might be all you ever have to do to meet the accessibility requirements for the language of the page.

However, if you have areas of your site where you have content in another language, you need to make sure it's wrapped in a lang tag so it's clear that the language is no longer the default.

For example, if you have a page that is defaulted to English and you shift to Spanish for a passage, you will use the lang tag along with a span tag like this (NOTE: You'll have to use the "text" or "html" view of the page to insert this).

This part of the page is defaulted to English. <span lang="es">Esta parte de la página está en español.</span> And now it's back to English.

While the words alone might signal to those reading visually that the language switches to Spanish, for those using assistive technology, having the language tag in place ensures that the text renders correctly. You can find the two-letter code for languages at www.iso.org/iso-639-language-codes.html.

Your Next Step

Review your current website content: Check the admin for your site builder and make sure the correct language is specified there. If you know you've got areas of the site where you change language from the default, you should also add the language tags to those passages to ensure they're read correctly by assistive technology.

For Future Content

Website and emails: Once your default site language is set, you won't have to think about that. Going forward, if you've got parts of your content in a different language, you'll just want to make sure that you have that wrapped in a lang tag. Even in emails, you should be able to add a language tag by editing the HTML of the content block (if needed, consult your email platform's help documentation for more details on editing HTML.)

Social media: This is not applicable for social media posts.

Who Benefits?

Anyone who uses text-to-speech technology or any other type of technology that converts on-screen text to another format, such as braille, benefits from proper use of language tags to ensure the words are presented correctly.

WCAG References

Guideline: Readable / Success Criterion: 3.1.1 Language of Page

Guideline: Readable / Success Criterion: 3.1.2 Language of Parts

8. AUDIO & VIDEO

MAKING audio and video presentations accessible adds to the time, and possibly the cost, to produce. These are steps you must take, however, so everyone has a good, inclusive experience with your multimedia content, whether it's on your site, linked from your newsletter, or presented on social media.

Here are the requirements for any audio or video you create. The goal is to always present the information in an alternative format to make sure it's available to everyone.

Transcripts for Audio-Only Programs

Examples include:

- A podcast.
- A recording of a speech or any other spoken word.
- Any audio presentation that has no video accompaniment.

For these types of programs, you must provide a full transcript that includes the spoken words and the identification of who is speaking. In addition, any other important audio information—such as sound effects or vocal tone/inflection—that is necessary to understand the content should also be present.

There are many services available where you can send files to be transcribed by an actual person so that you get a completed transcript back, which should be fairly accurate. As with any content you plan to release, you should absolutely proofread it to make sure it is accurate since an additional set of eyes before publication helps to ensure the quality.

There is also software available, such as Descript, which Jeff uses for the multimedia he creates, that you can use to have audio transcribed by artificial intelligence (A.I.). If you're using any type of A.I. for transcriptions, you must take the time to edit what the A.I. provides.

At best, A.I. is 95% accurate and it will get words wrong, especially names and any words that are less common. If the speaker is talking too fast or with an accent, the rate of errors can increase. In addition, A.I. can have difficulty with proper punctuation and capitalization.

A.I. Versus Edited Transcript

Here's an example from a *Big Gay Fiction Podcast* episode showing the difference between an A.I.-generated transcript and the final transcript that was published.

A.I. version:
Austin and Caleb are so cute as they, I each other. Take interest and ultimately spend some time talking about all the things they love about writing on actual paper. Sadly, it's only a meat cute.

Final version:

And Austin and Caleb are so cute as they eye each other, take interest, and ultimately spend some time talking about all the things they love about writing on actual paper. Sadly, it's only a meet cute.

In just those few sentences, there are many issues corrected by Jeff between the A.I. and final versions, including punctuation, sentence structure, missing words, and wrong words. So, just to reiterate, you must *always* edit A.I.-generated transcripts for accuracy.

Once you've got the transcript ready, you can add it to the page where the audio program is. Many podcasts, for example, place the transcript on the same page as the embedded audio and the links for what's discussed in an episode. If you put the transcript on a different page and have a link to it on the page where the audio is, that is fine as long as the transcript follows accessibility guidelines.

Captions for Audio/Video Programs

Examples include:

- Any video that has spoken words.
- Any video without spoken words that has sound effects, music, or other sounds that are required to understand the content.

Anytime you're working with video, you need to consider the captions in the same way an audio-only program requires transcripts.

The captions appear on screen, synchronized with the audio that's playing in the video, and provide the audio information in text format—all the spoken words, important sound effects, types of music playing, and anything else someone would need to understand the program's audio from only reading the captions.

There are two caption types:

Closed captions: These can be turned on and off by the user through a toggle that's usually found alongside the other controls on a video player.

Open captions: These captions are part of the video and can't be turned on and off by the viewer. Open captions are less preferable because they may obscure what's showing in the video.

It's also important to note that viewers prefer to be in control of the captions, so use open captions only if absolutely necessary, for example in a scenario where closed captions aren't available.

Creating captions requires much the same work as a transcript. However, you'll have to take additional steps to ensure the captions are synced to the video correctly.

Here are some tips:

The "sidecar" file: As with transcripts, you can send your video to a service that will have a human create the caption file, what's known as a "sidecar" file, for you.

If you're using software like Descript for audio/video editing, it can also create the sidecar file from the transcript it produces (and that you have corrected so it's accurate). Sidecar files come in different formats, with .srt and .vtt among the most common. YouTube and Vimeo both accept .srt and .vtt files.

Auto-generated captions: YouTube automatically creates captions for any video you upload and don't provide a sidecar file for (at this writing, Vimeo has an auto-generation feature that is only available to its Enterprise tier subscribers).

Depending on how long your video is, it may take a few hours for it to generate the captions. Once the auto-generation is done, you can return to YouTube to edit the captions for accuracy.

Also, as a note on YouTube, you can enter your script or edited transcript and YouTube will automatically sync it to the audio track.

Don't forget about captions on social media. Facebook, Instagram, TikTok, and others have auto-captioning options for videos and the possibility to edit them for accuracy. Make sure you're taking the time to correct anything that's auto-generated. If you're unsure how, check the "help" section for the platform.

Color choice and font size: An additional factor to keep in mind as you're adding captions to platforms like TikTok and Instagram is to pick easy-to-read colors and fonts for your captions. Consider the guidance we give in the "Use of Color/Color Contrast" section.

Meanwhile, by default on YouTube and other video platforms, the captions will be added with the standard black background and white text.

Optional transcripts: Speaking of transcripts in this context, it can be helpful for some of your audience to read a transcript rather than the captions in a video. So, while it's not required to provide a transcript for a video, consider offering it. Anytime there's an option to offer more choice in how content is consumed, it's better to do so.

Indicate why videos may have no captions: If you've got a video that has no spoken audio or sound that would be meaningful to understand the video, you should state why there are no captions present. This allows viewers to know that you haven't forgotten the captions. There are a couple of ways you can do this:

- **In the video's description:** On the page the video is displayed on—which could be the page or post on YouTube, Vimeo, Facebook, etc., or the page on your website where you've embedded the video—you can have a message that there are no captions because the video is silent. This detail can be added to any other description of the video you're displaying.
- **As a caption:** You could also create an actual caption to be displayed if viewers turn on captions. It could be as simple as "No captions present. No spoken words in video." or "No captions present. Only instrumental music playing." Something like that will allow viewers to understand what's available and why.

Don't discount the importance of captions to your entire audience. According to a study done in 2019 by Verizon Media and Publicis Media, 80% of respondents said they're more likely to watch an entire video with captions.[1] Further, research has shown that 80% of people who use captions aren't deaf or hard of hearing.[2] You can't afford not to do proper captions on every video you post since that's the primary way some people will get the audio information from the video.

When Auto-generated Captions are Okay

Live video programming is our one exception to the rule to not rely on captions that are automatically generated. If you're doing live video, we encourage you to use a platform that allows for live auto captions (Zoom, for example, offers this). While the live captions won't be perfect, they will allow members of your audience with hearing loss to have a better understanding of the live presentation.

Remember what E.M. Lindsey said in the "Accessing Content on the Web" section, that they had missed out on educational opportunities because captions weren't available during the live webinar session. Of course, for any replays from the live session, you'll want to provide properly edited and accurate captions.

Descriptions for Videos

The descriptions we're talking about here are to describe the visual content of a video. In the same way you add meaningful alternative text for an image so that those who can't perceive the image visually have the necessary information, you need to provide descriptive information for videos.

Beyond the imagery in the video that might need descriptions, you absolutely need an alternative way to provide any text that appears on screen as the video plays.

Of the items in this section, this is the most difficult. However, there are a few ways to handle the descriptions:

In the spoken script: Include any important visual information right in the script for the words that are spoken. Not only should your script include all the text that appears on screen but as much of the other visual information as possible.

On the web page: Adjacent to the video on the web page, write text that describes the important visual information in the video, including any text that appears on screen. If you're providing this equivalent information, visitors will understand what you're conveying in the video even if they can't visually perceive it.

Descriptive transcript: You can take the above one step

further and create a descriptive transcript that details all the important visual information. This should include a time stamp for each item described so it's understood where in the video the information is displayed. This transcript can also include the audio information, if any, so it becomes an even more complete transcript.

You'll find an example of a descriptive transcript on our website where we explain how to use the WAVE browser extension at ContentForEveryone.info/book/scan/.

Audio description: Providing an audio description track is the most ideal way to provide descriptions unless you're already describing everything in the audio.

You may have noticed audio descriptions provided for programs airing on TV and via streaming apps by using a secondary audio track that plays alongside the program's primary audio. In this scenario, the descriptions of on-screen visuals are spoken in between the dialogue.

While this is the best way to go, it can be a challenge for creative entrepreneurs.

At this writing, YouTube, Vimeo, and social media platforms don't offer the ability to upload a secondary audio track to use for the audio descriptions. YouTube has been in beta with a new function to upload secondary audio, but it's not clear when it will become available for all.

Of course, even if you can upload a secondary track, there's still the matter of creating one. That might be technically difficult for creators, who would have to write and record a track that aligns well with the primary audio so there's no overlapping dialogue between the program's main speakers and the descriptive information.

As an alternative to uploading a secondary track, you can create another version of the video that includes the audio description track within the primary audio track so that anyone playing the video always hears both.

Your Next Step

Review your current website content: You probably already know the extent to which you've used transcripts, captions, and descriptions in the past, so you may not need to conduct an overall review. If you do, you'll need to go to the page where the media appears and check what's present.

This is another area where you'll have to consider how much content you've created and if you can spend the time and money to add captions and transcripts or if you will only create them going forward. If you have a lot of legacy content where these elements are not available, you may want to put that information into your accessibility statement so visitors know what to expect.

For Future Content

Website and social media: As you're creating new multimedia, make sure you're adding time and/or the budget to have it transcribed and captioned correctly, including the correction of any auto-generated material.

If you're doing a video, make it easy on yourself and ensure your script includes any important text that appears on screen and a description of any important activities that are demonstrated.

Emails: This isn't applicable for emails since you likely aren't embedding audio and video directly into emails. Instead, you'll be linking from emails to websites where you'll be managing the multimedia accessibility.

Who Benefits?

Everyone: Transcripts and captions have value for everyone as these options allow for the text to be read rather than listened to.

For a transcript, this can be great for users who want to skim content quickly or who may be searching for something they'd heard previously and want to find it in text rather than having to listen to a complete program.

For captions, these are useful for anyone who might be watching a video in an environment where playing the audio isn't convenient. Captions can also help non-native language speakers understand the content better by providing written text of the spoken words.

Visually impaired: Text alternatives for visual content, such as descriptions of video images, help people who have difficulty perceiving the content.

In addition, those text alternatives can be converted into other forms, including speech and braille. Audio descriptions of the visual content also allow these visitors to understand the visual information.

Cognitively impaired: The text-based alternatives aid people who may have difficulty understanding audio or video content. This is the case for transcripts, captions, and descriptions because they allow the user to choose the best way to engage with the content.

Auditory impaired: Text alternatives allow people who have any kind of hearing loss to access the content. In the case of captions, it allows the audio information to be presented in sync with the video.

WCAG References

Guideline: Time-Based Media / Success Criterion: 1.2.1
Audio-only and Video-only (Pre-recorded)
Guideline: Time-Based Media / Success Criterion: 1.2.2
Captions (Pre-recorded)
Guideline: Time-Based Media / Success Criterion: 1.2.3
Audio Description or Media Alternative (Pre-recorded)
Guideline: Time-Based Media / Success Criterion: 1.2.4
Captions (Live)
Guideline: Time-Based Media / Success Criterion: 1.2.5
Audio Description (Pre-recorded)

9. SEIZURES

CERTAINLY, you will not set out to create content that can cause anyone to have seizures or any kind of physical reaction. However, it is possible to create an animated image or video that can cause problems for some of your site visitors.

Seizures and physical reactions can happen if there is content with flashes that occur three or more times in a single second. There is even more possibility for a reaction if the colors are a combination of white, yellow, and/or red.

What likely comes to mind first when you think about this kind of rapid flashing is a strobe light. This is why live performance venues post warnings about the use of strobes. Streaming services also routinely post content warnings when programs have explosions or other flashes that may cause a reaction for some viewers.

In most cases, we would advise you to simply avoid flashing content to ensure you're doing no harm. However, if flashes are important, make sure they are under the three-per-second threshold.

While the Web Content Accessibility Guidelines do not

mention images that can cause seizures, it's important to know that those exist so that you can avoid using them.[1] These types of images include patterns such as a zigzag, black-and-white bars in a pattern, multiple wavy lines, and other image types that are referred to as "grating images."

Your Next Step

Review your current website and social media content: Depending on how large your site is, you may not easily be able to search out all the media you've posted that might include flashing.

If you think you have included any, please, at a minimum, locate it and put a warning on it or remove it altogether. You should do the same for your social media content if you think any of it might have flashes or images that might cause harm.

For Future Content

Website, emails, and social media: Now that you know what kind of visuals can cause seizures and physical reactions, you can ensure that you're not using them.

Who Benefits?

Everyone: Avoiding content, or at a minimum advising on content, that may cause visitors to have a physical reaction, or even worse a seizure, will ensure that your content doesn't create a potentially harmful scenario.

Photosensitive visitors: They are the group that is most susceptible to seizures caused by flashing content or grating images.

WCAG Reference

Guideline: Seizures / Success Criterion: 2.3.1 Three Flashes or Below Threshold

10. AUTO PLAY ELEMENTS: CAROUSELS, VIDEOS, ANIMATIONS

IF YOU HAVE anything on your site that begins playing or moving automatically or that automatically updates the page with new content, we suggest you review its use and make sure it's accessible for all users.

There are two areas specifically to check for:

Auto-start content: Anything on the site that starts automatically, lasts more than five seconds, and is alongside other content must have a way for it to be paused, stopped, and/or hidden unless the movement is essential (in our experience, the movement is rarely essential).

Content that falls into this category includes carousels, animated GIFs, and multimedia programs. This rule extends to anything that's moving, blinking, or scrolling.

Auto-updating content: If any content on the site updates automatically, such as new content that appears on the page and changes the position of existing content, and those updates start playing automatically, users must also have a way to start, stop, or hide the updates.

Auto-updating content usually turns up on social media sites as new posts come into the timeline, and on news sites as reports come in on breaking news stories. It's not likely a feature that you're using, but if it is, please make sure proper start, stop, and hide controls are available and that they are labeled properly and accessible to all users.

Some of these automatic elements might be easier to manage than others.

Videos: Whether a video plays automatically is usually a setting in the video player that you can choose as you're embedding. You should always choose to not allow the video to auto play. In addition, make sure that you're embedding videos with all the controls available in the player.

At all times you want your visitors to be in control of the content. If you need more details on the options you have when you're embedding videos, check the help documentation available with the platform you're using.

Audio: As with video player embeds mentioned above, you'll find the same options regarding auto play for any audio that you're embedding on the site. Again, make sure the content is not set to auto play.

Image carousels: The controls and settings will vary depending on the theme or plug-in you use to create the carousel. There are a few features you should make sure the carousel has:

- A setting so it doesn't start rotating or sliding automatically, or if it does, the user has access to a control to stop it.
- Visible left and right controls (such as arrows) so users can move between panels.
- Ideally, an indication for the user on how many panels are in the carousel.

For carousels, also consider the topics we've covered in

previous sections as well. You'll want to use a carousel that accepts a combination of images and text so that you don't have to rely on images of text. The carousel also needs a way for you to enter alternative text for any images used.

It might be a challenge to find a carousel that has all the controls properly labeled for assistive technologies as well as controls that can be used only with a keyboard. You'll want to understand, as best as you can, the accessibility of the carousel before using it.

Your Next Step

Review your current website content: Each of these is a specialty item and you'll need to review each instance you have on your website. Often there are only a handful of carousels on a website, and you can review those when you make updates to them.

However, for the other items, especially animations and auto-play videos that might be on older blog posts or pages, this will be another case where you must weigh the time of finding and updating them versus the overall benefit.

For Future Content

Website and emails: Consider if you really need to use anything that starts on its own and continues to play. If you decide to use such an item, make sure to follow our guidance. If you're using animations (such as GIFs) for visual interest, make sure they're set to stop playing after one cycle or that the user has a way to stop them.

If you're using animations in emails, consult the help documentation for your email platform to see what controls are available so that the recipients can stop them.

Social media: This is not applicable for social media posts as the platforms typically have settings available for the user to decide if they want content to auto play or to repeat.

Who Benefits?

Visually impaired: Moving text can cause disruptions to screen readers if content is moved from the focus before the user has finished interacting with it. Moving and blinking content can also be difficult for users with low vision who may need more time with the content or who may have issues reading content that isn't stationary.

Cognitively impaired: For visitors with some cognitive impairments, such as attention deficit, content that is moving in any way can distract them from being able to complete the task they came to the website for. For others, moving content can make the information more difficult to understand because it is not static.

WCAG Reference
Guideline: Enough Time / Success Criterion: 2.2.2 Pause, Stop, Hide

11. KEYBOARD NAVIGATION, FOCUS ORDER & VISIBLE FOCUS

HAVE you ever tried to navigate a website on your computer without the use of a mouse or other pointing device (such as a trackball or trackpad)? You should be able to navigate to and use every interactive item—a link, button, form field, etc.—using only your keyboard.

The same is true if you were to attach a keyboard to a mobile phone or tablet. Rather than touching the screen on those devices, the attached keyboard must allow navigation to those same interactive items.

The ability to keyboard navigate is also critical for users of assistive technology like screen readers, which rely on a site having correct keyboard navigation. In this book, however, we're not going to cover the specialized keyboard navigating that screen reader users have available to them on computers and mobile devices.

The tab key is the primary one used in keyboard navigation. Pressing tab moves the focus from one interactive element to the next, such as link to link, form field to form field, and so on.

Depending on the type of element, other keys are used to

interact with it. For example, when you tab to a link, you press "Enter" to activate the link and proceed to the destination. For more detail on the keys that are used to interact with elements on a page, go to ContentForEveryone.info/book/keyboard.

Keyboard navigation is not an easy item for you to manage on your own unless you're a developer, but it's important to understand because it can impact how people interact with your website.

You shouldn't encounter an issue with the basics of this requirement unless you've had some custom development done that prohibits keyboard navigation from working correctly or you're using a theme or plug-in that is poorly built.

There are additional items to consider alongside keyboard navigation.

Focus order: The order in which a user moves through the site via keyboard must be logical, moving in the natural reading order (for example, in English that would be from left to right and top to bottom), and in an order that makes sense for the meaning and operation of the content.

You wouldn't, for example, want the focus to jump from the top of the page to the bottom and back to the middle again.

This can get more complicated if pop-ups are involved as well since focus should be brought to a pop-up as soon as it appears. As with keyboard navigation, this should just work.

Visible focus: There must be a visible focus indicator, such as an outline around the item, to show which interactive element is selected as someone moves through the site with the tab key. Imagine the frustration if there was no way to know which link was selected as you moved through the site.

The color of the focus indicator must also follow the non-text contrast rule so that it stands out from the site's background enough to be visible to everyone.

Depending on your platform, you can find plug-ins that can add a focus indicator to your site. If you've had a site custom built, you'll need to go back to your developer if they didn't add an indicator.

If you've never tried to keyboard navigate through a website, try it on a few different sites and you'll quickly understand the frustration if you can't understand where the focus indicator is or if the focus order jumps around in an illogical way. We also have an example of visible focus indicators at ContentforEveryone.info/book/focus.

Your Next Step

Review your current website content: After a page loads, start tabbing through the site. The order should go from left to right and top to bottom, stopping on each interactive element—a link, form field, or another item you can interact with.

If you've got multiple columns on your site, the correct ordering would be to go left to right and top to bottom beginning in the leftmost column and repeating that with each column to the right.

As you're tabbing, there should be a visible focus indicator—it could be a box around the item, an underline, or something else to let you know where the focus is.

For Future Content

Website: Unless you change your template after you've reviewed its functions or you add a new type of page, you shouldn't have to think about this.

However, since templates are often updated by their creators, you may want to check this periodically to make sure nothing unexpected has changed.

Emails: You should find that your email platform manages the focus order and indicator. If you use a custom HTML template, you should work with the developer to make sure the focus order and focus indicator are managed correctly.

Social media: This is not applicable for social media posts as keyboard navigation is set by the platform.

Who Benefits?

Everyone: Anyone might prefer keyboard navigation, so make sure the rules for keyboard navigation are followed so the experience is good.

Visually impaired: People who are blind rely on keyboard navigation and proper focus order since they cannot use a mouse or any other device that relies on hand-eye coordination.

People with low vision or other vision impairments may use keyboard navigation because they may have difficulty locating or following a pointer on screen.

Motor impaired: Visitors with arthritis or other motor difficulties may be unable to use a mouse or interact with a touch screen, making keyboard navigation something they may need to use.

Cognitively impaired: People with short-term memory difficulties or attention deficit may need the visual focus indicator to remind them of their place on the page. Using keyboard navigation may also help them focus attention better than using a mouse.

WCAG References

Guideline: Distinguishable / Success Criterion: 1.4.11 Non-text Contrast

Guideline: Keyboard Navigation / Success Criterion: 2.1.1 Keyboard

Guideline: Navigable / Success Criterion: 2.4.3 Focus Order

Guideline: Navigable / Success Criterion: 2.4.7 Focus Visible

12. INSTRUCTIONS, LABELS & ERROR MESSAGES

THESE ITEMS GO TOGETHER because they all revolve around making sure your visitors understand what's needed to accomplish actions when interacting with forms on your site, such as leaving a comment, signing up for a newsletter, or making a purchase.

How difficult these are to manage will vary, and sometimes you may not be able to do it on your own. We do, however, want to make you aware of these items in case you receive feedback from your site visitors about them or if you're working with a developer who can help you review them.

Let's break down the three elements:

Instructions: This will be the easiest for most content creators as you should be able to add any needed instructions on your site with minimal difficulties.

Where it can be more complex is if you need to add additional information within plug-ins or widgets. If that's the case, you may need to add additional details next to those items on the page or even link to another page to provide details.

Clear instructions, including any specific formats that visitors need to use to enter information (such as dates or phone numbers), are critical so it's clear what needs to be entered into forms and how to perform site functions in order to avoid mistakes.

Labels: Every form field on the site, regardless of its purpose, should have clear labeling. Those labels aren't only related to what is visually available on the screen, but those same labels need to be available to screen readers and anyone using assistive technology.

Further, the visible form field's label should match the accessible name (i.e., the code element "label" that is used to associate the form field with the name announced by a screen reader) the developers set in the code in case someone is navigating by speaking to their device.

Unfortunately, sometimes developers don't align the names. What shows as "First Name" on screen might be "FName" or even an empty label in the code.

Poor labeling can cause many issues, including not being able to fill out the form at all. Unless you're a developer, however, you won't be able to review and fix these items.

Error messages: Another item that will be nearly impossible to fix unless you're a developer will be to make any adjustments to error messages that are presented.

It's important to have clear error messages so users who make mistakes have information on where they are and how to correct them.

If you can't change error messages, consider providing more and clearer instructional copy so users can avoid the errors. When presenting error messages, it's also important to make sure they're perceivable by all, such as using a combination of color, icons, and understandable text.

Further, each error message should be linked to its associated input. However, this is something you'll only be able to review and fix with the help of a developer as there is specific coding needed.

Your Next Step

Review your current website content: For the instructions and error messages, review the areas of your site where there are forms for users to fill out.

Check the instructions that are present to determine if they are clear and understandable. You can also fill out the form yourself and make mistakes so you can review the error messages that are present.

The labels are going to be more complex and unless you're a developer or skilled with assistive technology like a screen reader, it'll be difficult for you to review these. This might be a review you'd want to skip unless you're working with a developer or you get feedback from a site visitor that they're having trouble.

For Future Content

Website: Once you've done the review of your current configuration, you won't need to do this again unless you're adding a new component that has instructions and error messages or if you do other updates where the configuration might change.

Emails and social media: This is not applicable for emails and social media posts.

Who Benefits?

Everyone: Clear instructions, messaging, and labeling are good for everyone to ensure they understand what is required when filling out forms or taking other actions on your site.

Visually impaired: Providing information about errors as plain text ensures blind, color blind, and other visually impaired users have access to information in ways they can perceive.

Cognitively impaired: Plain text instructions help people with cognitive impairments understand what's required to fill out forms and how to avoid and correct errors.

Motor impaired: For visitors who might use speech-to-text technology to speak commands, ensuring fields are labeled correctly and match the visual label is important to make sure the form can be used. Good instructions and error messaging also means fewer movements overall while filling out forms.

WCAG References

Guideline: Navigable / Success Criterion: 2.4.6 Headings & Labels

Guideline: Input Assistance / Success Criterion: 3.3.1 Error Identification

Guideline: Input Assistance / Success Criterion: 3.3.2 Labels or Instructions

Guideline: Input Assistance / Success Criterion: 3.3.3 Error Suggestion

Guideline: Robust / Success Criterion: 4.1.2 Name, Role, Value

13. POP-UP WINDOWS

POP-UP WINDOWS, such as what are often used for newsletter sign-ups, special notifications of sales or events, and cookie policy information to name a few, can present challenges if they are not integrated correctly in the page.

We'd recommend against using pop-ups of any kind if you can avoid them since they'll be quite difficult for you to fix without the help of a skilled developer. Another option is finding a plug-in or theme that has accessible pop-ups.

Among the most important issues to watch out for with pop-ups:

Proper focus: We've found many instances where pop-ups appear but they don't receive focus, meaning users of assistive technologies like screen readers won't know the pop-up is present.

Keyboard navigation: While the pop-up is on screen, keyboard navigation should be restricted to the pop-up until the functions are completed or the user dismisses the pop-up. If the navigation is allowed to leave the pop-up, the user might not be able to get back to the pop-up and might end up navigating behind it.

Like all complex components, there are multiple items to review when evaluating the accessibility of pop-ups, but for the purpose of this guide we only focused on the Operable principle for the Keyboard and Navigable guidelines. You'll also want to check the accessibility of the content that is presented inside the pop-up just as you would for a full web page.

Your Next Step

Review your current website content: Review all the pop-ups on your site. When the pop-up displays, the user should be able to tab through all the interactive components (i.e., any form fields and buttons).

Usually pop-ups have an "X" somewhere to close (and some will have a "close" or "exit" link or button). Make sure that you can navigate to those with the keyboard.

Speaking of the "X," if you press "enter" or "space," does that make the pop-up close? It should. The pop-up should also close if you press the escape key.

The experience you want to avoid is for the pop-up to appear and, as you tab, you find that you're moving around on the page behind the pop-up. If that happens or if the tests above fail, we recommend you find another pop-up that is accessible.

For Future Content

Website: Ideally, you won't introduce any new pop-ups to your site. If you do, make sure you follow our guidance to ensure you're adding one that is accessible.

Emails and social media: This is not applicable for emails and social media posts.

Who Benefits?

Everyone: Any user who wishes to use keyboard navigation will appreciate that pop-ups receive proper focus.

Visually impaired: If pop-ups aren't working correctly, blind users who navigate via a screen reader may not be able to access them or might become trapped if pop-ups don't close via keyboard.

Cognitively impaired: Pop-ups might be a distraction for some members of your audience, especially those with cognitive disabilities like ADHD.

As Karla Hailer mentioned in the "Accessing Content on the Web" section, she will leave a site that has too many distractions, such as marketing pop-ups. If you're using pop-ups, make sure they're relevant and that you're not using too many.

Motor impaired: These users are most likely to use keyboard navigation or other means of navigation and will be negatively impacted if they cannot navigate the pop-up correctly.

WCAG References

Guideline: Navigable / Success Criterion: 1.3.1 Info and Relationships

Guideline: Navigable / Success Criterion: 1.3.2 Meaningful Sequence

Guideline: Keyboard Navigation / Success Criterion: 2.1.1 Keyboard

Guideline: Navigable / Success Criterion: 2.4.3 Focus Order

Guideline: Navigable / Success Criterion: 2.4.6 Headings & Labels

Guideline: Navigable / Success Criterion: 2.4.7 Focus Visible

14. CONSISTENCY

Providing a consistent experience is helpful to everyone who visits your site. In many cases, WordPress, Wix, and other platforms have themes to make it easy to offer consistent navigation across the site for the header and footer.

Those same themes also allow you to set it up so that any sidebars you may create have the same elements across some or all of the pages.

Ensuring that repeated components occur in the same place and with the same ordering allows for easier navigation through the site.

You can also extend this concept to the layout of your pages. For example, if you've got pages about your creations, such as books, music, jewelry, paintings, pottery, whatever it is, you can showcase the items in a consistent way across the pages.

If you're an author and have a page for each of your books, each page could contain the cover, the blurb, links to purchase, reviews, and an excerpt. Placing those elements in the same location on the page for each book makes it easy for your visitors to find the information they want without having to reorient themselves to a new page layout.

In addition to a consistent navigation, it's also beneficial to have a consistency in the identification of elements and sections of pages.

Consider a newsletter sign-up form where on one page the button to submit the email address reads "sign up now," and on another page reads "subscribe now," and on still another reads "submit." The same function labeled three different ways across the site could cause confusion.

Your Next Step

Review your current website content: Review your navigation elements and confirm they're consistent across the site (they probably are unless you've done custom work on your theme).

Also check the content for any pages you have that are presenting similar types of information (such as product pages) and strive to create consistency there as well.

For Future Content

Website: Follow the consistency you've established when creating new content.

Emails: Considering how templatized email platforms are, you're probably already being consistent in presentation for your emails, which makes it easy for your audience to engage with each email you send. If you're not being consistent, look to change that in your future emails.

Social media: This is not applicable for social media posts since this type of content is expected to be more free-form.

Who Benefits?

Everyone: Having consistent navigation, identification, and content organization makes engaging with content easier because visitors won't have to reorient themselves on common elements.

Visually impaired: Having repeated components in the same order on each page helps users who are blind or with low vision to be able to predict where elements are on a page.

Consistent identification helps those who rely on the labels, such as through a screen reader, to be able to search and find needed functions.

It also allows users to skip sections of the website once they understand the organizational structure. For example, they can confidently skip the navigation bar and go directly to content.

Cognitively impaired: This group is also assisted by being able to predict where elements are on pages. In addition, when things are identified in a consistent way, they can quickly find elements on page throughout the site.

Motor impaired: Consistent navigation and identification allows users to make less movement to achieve their goals. Further, if they're using speech to navigate a site, the consistency helps the accuracy of that navigation.

WCAG References
Guideline: Navigable / Success Criterion: 3.2.3 Consistent Navigation
Guideline: Navigable / Success Criterion: 3.2.4 Consistent Identification

15. TABLES

TABLES full of data are among the most difficult things to make accessible. It's possible you may not have a need to use them in your content, but sometimes you might decide a table is needed to present information like sizing charts, schedule information, or feature comparisons.

There are many reasons to use them, and if you're going to, you need to think about accessibility to ensure everyone in your audience can access the information.

Fundamentally, everything you include in a table needs to be accessible on its own following the guidance we've offered throughout the "Practical Guide."

So, if you're including images, those need to have meaningful alternative text and you should avoid images of text.

If there are colors in the chart that are supposed to have meaning—perhaps green to indicate something is available and red to indicate it's not—you also need to present equivalent information in text for those who can't perceive the color.

Where tables get trickier is how assistive technologies interact with them. In some cases, charts need to be read column by column but for others it's row by row. The data needs to be read in a certain order and needs to be presented in a logical way by the screen reader so that it makes sense when it's read out.

For site visitors with low vision, tables could be a challenge if they're using screen magnifiers and can't see enough of the table to be able to understand the data presented.

Members of your audience with cognitive impairments may also have difficulty parsing the data amongst all the rows and columns.

Should You Use Tables?

We don't want to tell you not to use something. Accessibility is not about restricting creativity around how content is presented. Sometimes, it's possible to allow data to be presented in a format that doesn't use a table. However, in other instances using a table might be essential and necessary to presenting data or complex information.

The issue is that making a table accessible requires someone with the skill to ensure it's coded correctly.

Even if you make the contents of the individual cells accessible, there's still the matter of how it would read out to screen readers and other assistive technologies. That's something that is likely outside your skill set.

Our best guidance is to consider the content you want to put into a table and determine if it can be presented in another format, such as a bulleted list.

You could also have the table and then link it to a page where the data is in an alternate format. The key is to make sure the information is available to everyone.

Your Next Step

Review your current website content: If you have any tables on your website, review them and decide if they can be replaced by presenting the content in a different format or if the table should stay as is with additional methods of presenting the information for those who need it. This might also be an instance where you want to consult with a developer to review if an essential table is properly accessible.

For Future Content

Website: As we noted earlier, if you're considering using a table, think about how that information might be presented in a different format where achieving accessibility will be easier.

Emails: Given the limited space in emails, we encourage avoiding the use of tables completely.

Social media: This is not applicable for social media posts.

Who Benefits?

Visually or cognitively impaired: These visitors will appreciate that you're presenting table content in an accessible way they can understand.

WCAG References

Guideline: Navigable / Success Criterion: 1.3.1 Info and Relationships

Guideline: Navigable / Success Criterion: 1.3.2 Meaningful Sequence

16. CLEAR, CONCISE, EASY TO READ CONTENT

WE IMAGINE everyone wants to write content that is easily understood by everyone. After all, simplicity is one of the best rules. Here are a few tips to keep in mind.

Sentence structure: Write in short, clear sentences and paragraphs.

Simplicity: Avoid using unnecessarily complex words and phrases. Don't mistake this to mean that you should not write about more complex topics. The point is to make your content easy to understand for the widest potential audience.

Acronym usage: Define all acronyms on first use. Even for common acronyms you should do this since you can't be sure that everyone will have the same understanding.

If your content has a lot of specialized terms and/or phrases, consider setting up a glossary page. A glossary will give your audience an easy reference point.

Lists: Use list formatting with bullets or numbers to help break up content. This can be an ideal way to organize content, especially if you're writing several short sentences.

Use headings: As we described in the "Headings" section, this ensures meaningfully organized content.

Information in multiple ways: Use images, illustrations, video, audio, icons, symbols, and other methods of communication to clarify and support your text.

It's never wrong to present information in multiple formats to ensure that everyone can perceive and understand it.

Font usage: Don't use fancy fonts. Keep the text easy to read with standard fonts. If you're using fancy fonts for branding or visual interest, present equivalent text in a standard font as well. The best fonts are ones that have strong, unique characters.

Avoid fonts where characters can be misunderstood, such as fonts where lowercase L, uppercase I, and the numeral 1 all have a similar appearance.

Among the fonts that are considered the most accessible are Tahoma, Times New Roman, and Verdana. Arial, Calibri, and Helvetica also have many accessible characteristics, although the lower case L and upper case I aren't as distinguishable as they are with other fonts. Be cautious with fonts that might indicate they are accessible but really are not.

Keep usage of italics and bold text to a minimum. Of course, you can italicize words and phrases for emphasis and to designate titles of books and TV shows. However, large blocks of italicized text can be a challenge to read. The same is true for bold text. Use it to draw attention to a few words or a phrase, or with a headline or subhead, but don't overuse it otherwise.

Text alignment: Align text to the left, rather than centering or justifying text. It takes more effort to read text when it doesn't begin at the same point on every line (as with centering) or if there are varying amounts of white space between words (as with justification).

Of course, you can center headlines or a small amount of text, but don't center entire paragraphs.

Readable font size: Make sure you're using font sizes that are readable for visitors who may have low vision. Even if you're writing "fine print" for giveaway rules or something similar, you should still ensure text is easily readable by anyone visiting the page.

Color contrast: Make sure all the text and non-text content has proper color contrast as we described in the "Use of Color/Color Contrast" section.

Your Next Step

Review your current website content: This is as easy as checking the content on your site, from the home page to key informational and product pages. If you've got a blog, perhaps review the most recent blog posts as well.

As with some other areas we've mentioned, if you have a lot of content, you might not dig too much into the past, but do what you can to make the content that gets the most traffic as easy to read as possible and then use best practices going forward.

For Future Content

Website, emails, and social media: Use these best practices for all new content you create.

Who Benefits?

Everyone: Truly everyone benefits when you present the clearest, easiest to understand content that you can.

SOCIAL MEDIA & EMAIL

THROUGHOUT THE "PRACTICAL Guide to Improving Your Content's Accessibility" section we highlighted areas important to social media and email, but we wanted to discuss these two areas further to help you create posts, newsletters, and other communications that are understandable for everyone.

Alternative text: Always follow the rules for alternative text we laid out in the "Images/Non-text Content" section. Your email provider should have a way for you to add alternative text to images you use in emails.

The social media platforms also allow you to add alternative text to images as you're posting, so take advantage of that. If you don't know where to enter the alternative text, consult the help information for the platforms you use.

Images of text: Be aware of how you use images with text in them. As we detailed in the "Images of Text" section, images of text are never accessible, and even if you add alternative text, not everyone will access that detail. Make sure you put the text from the image into your social post or adjacent to the image in an email so everyone gets equivalent information.

Images that are links: If you're adding links to images within newsletters, make sure the alternative text states where the link will go. We'd recommend avoiding linked images as much as possible because they can be unclear for many reasons. If you must have linked images, though, make sure the link destination is explicitly stated.

Overusing images in email: Please don't create an email that's all images. Even with good alternative text, there will be people in your audience who will not be able to understand because they don't process information from images as well as they would from text on the page. Use a mix of text and images that work together.

Clear, concise text: We offered tips for creating clear, concise, and easy-to-read content in a previous section, and doing this is even more important in social media. There's so much distraction on social media, so the clearer the message is the better the chance it can be understood and engaged with.

Hashtags: When you're using hashtags, don't put them in all lowercase. Use camel case, which is the use of a capital letter to begin the second and subsequent words, or pascal case, which is a capital letter to begin each word. It's much easier to read #thisIsAHashtag or #ThisIsAHashtag than #thisisahashtag.

Camel and pascal case allow screen readers to parse and present the words correctly, as they'll recognize a new word starting with the uppercase letter.

For anyone reading the hashtag, it'll also be much easier to figure out the words. Be careful on sites that try to auto-complete hashtags for you using lowercase, such as Instagram and LinkedIn. Make sure to add them with camel case or pascal case.

Emojis: Use emojis limitedly and thoughtfully. They look great as decoration at the end of a post but using too many can confuse some users who may not understand what the emoji is trying to convey. In addition, screen readers have very specific text that they'll read for each emoji, and it may not be what you mean.

For example, one of Jeff's favorite emoji combinations to use is a red heart, a rainbow pride flag, and a stack of books. He means for this to represent "love gay books." It visually looks good at the end of a social post about a book. However, if a screen reader read that out, it would be "red heart rainbow flag books." The meaning might be inferred, but perhaps not.

Something else to avoid is an emoji between each word of a headline or sentence. Imagine an emoji was displayed each time an "X" appears in the following: "X Limited X Time X Offer X."

If that emoji was a smiling face emoji a screen reader would read out: "Slightly Smiling Face Limited Slightly Smiling Face Time Slightly Smiling Face Offer Slightly Smiling Face."

That's painful to have read out by a screen reader. Meanwhile, for people visually reading the text, it could be difficult to parse out the actual message, not just the words but the meaning of the emojis in context.

WHAT CAN YOU FIND WITH
AN ACCESSIBILITY SCAN?

THROUGHOUT THE "PRACTICAL GUIDE" section, we told you how you can check for each of the items on your website. There's another activity you can do that will allow you to identify some accessibility issues.

While an automated scan doesn't provide a comprehensive snapshot of the accessibility of your site, it can give you meaningful information to help you understand some aspects of accessibility.

For this task, WAVE, a web accessibility evaluation tool available from WebAIM, is a commonly used tool. It's a free browser extension available at wave.webaim.org and there are versions available for Chrome, Firefox, and Edge.

It's simple to run a scan by going to the page you want to analyze and triggering the browser extension.

The report structures the information, classifying the findings as "errors," "contrast errors," "alerts," "features," "structural elements," and "ARIA." [1]

In each of these sections, there's the possibility you will find many items reported. We're going to focus on the items WAVE reports that are also things we tell you how to check.

Again, please don't take the scan information as the only review you should perform. Checking each item as we suggest in the "Practical Guide" section should still be done.

Errors

Here's what WAVE reports in the "errors" section that relates to what we covered in the "Practical Guide" section:

Image without an alt attribute: This specifically checks if an image has an alt attribute present, which is required. It can't tell you if the alternative text is meaningful, and it cannot recommend if the alt attribute should be empty because the image is decorative. (You can find more about how to manage this issue in the "Images/Non-text Content" section.)

Linked image, image map, or image button without alternative text: These are three different yet important items. If there are images (including image maps) that are links, or images that are used for buttons, they must have good alternative text that describes the function of the image and the link destination. (You can find more about how to manage this issue in the "Images/Non-text Content" section.)

Spacer images missing alternative text: All images must have an alt attribute, including ones that are used for spacers or that might be invisible. In these cases, the alt attribute should be empty. You might not be able to fix these depending on your theme and plug-ins, but it's good to know if there are issues with these. (You can find more about how to manage this issue in the "Images/Non-text Content" section.)

Missing/uninformative page title: Unique page titles are important, and while this scan can't tell you if your title is meaningful, this will indicate if it's missing, contains only spaces, or starts with "untitled." (You can find more about how to manage this issue in the "Page Titles" section.)

Language missing/invalid: This will let you know if the default language of your page is set and if it's set with a valid language code. It will not tell you if you've set it to the correct language, though. (You can find more about how to manage this issue in the "Language of the Page/Parts of the Page" section.)

Empty heading: This will tell you if you're using a heading tag, such as H1, H2, etc., as a blank line, which would need to be corrected. (You can find more about how to manage this issue in the "Headings" section.)

Empty link: This means the link has no text associated with it. It's unlikely you'd have this, but if this error crops up, identify the link and remove it or provide text for it. (You can find more about how to manage this issue in the "Link Text" section.)

Blinking content: It's very late 1990s to make things blink, so hopefully you're not doing this. If you are, though, you should remove it since it falls under what we talked about related to being able to pause, stop, and hide auto play elements. (You can find more about how to manage this issue in the "Auto Play Elements: Carousels, Videos, Animations" section.)

Low contrast: WAVE will report if there's text on the page that doesn't meet color contrast requirements. (You can find more about how to manage this issue in the "Use of Color/Color Contrast" section.)

Alerts

In addition to "errors" that need to be fixed, WAVE can also tell you where you should review what's on the page more closely. Here are some categories we recommend you search for in the "alerts" section so you can check the details that WAVE provides:

Alternative text: While WAVE can't tell you specifically if text is meaningful, it can tell you if it seems suspicious in some way, if you've got redundant alternative text on the page, or if it's too long. (You can find more about how to manage this issue in the "Images/Non-text Content" section.)

Headings: Again, it can't tell you if you're organizing the content on the page well, but you'll get notified if there's no heading structure or if you've skipped heading levels. (You can find more about how to manage this issue in the "Headings" section.)

Links: WAVE gives feedback if it appears link text may not make sense out of context and if there are redundant links on the page. (You can find more about how to manage this issue in the "Link Text" section.)

Multimedia: While it's probably easy for you to spot if there is audio and video on your pages, you'll be alerted here so that you can review the accessibility of the media. (You can find more about how to manage this issue in the "Audio & Video" section.)

Text: If there's text that might be too small for visitors with low vision, or if you're using text alignments or styles that may cause accessibility issues, you'll be alerted. (You can find more about how to manage this issue in the "Clear, Concise, Easy to Read Content" section.)

Features

Under "features" are a couple of additional things you can review. In these instances, they're items that appear to be correctly present, but WAVE flags them so you can make sure. Here are the issue types you should check:

Alternative text: Yes, we mention it again here. WAVE flags the alternative text on the page so you can review if what you have is appropriate and meaningful. (You can find more about how to manage this issue in the "Images/Non-text Content" section.)

Language tag: Make sure the default language of the site that WAVE reports is the correct language. (You can find more about how to manage this issue in the "Language of the Page/Parts of the Page" section.)

Structure

Lastly is the "structure" section and there are a few things here you can check:

Headings: WAVE will let you know what headings are on the page so you can decide if you need to make adjustments. (You can find more about how to manage this issue in the "Headings" section.)

Ordered lists: If there's a numbered list present, it will flag it so you can check its correctness. (You can find more about how to manage this issue in the "Clear, Concise, Easy to Read Content" section.)

Unordered lists: As with the ordered lists, you can review these as well. (You can find more about how to manage this issue in the "Clear, Concise, Easy to Read Content" section.)

As noted, in each of the categories above, it's likely WAVE will call out issue types we haven't mentioned. In addition, WAVE also has the ARIA section, which doesn't contain items we'd recommend for your review.

If you want to get any of the other issues reviewed and/or

fixed, we believe you'll need to work with a professional developer who is skilled in accessibility and the platform you're using to help you.

For a brief video demonstration on how to use WAVE on a website, go to ContentForEveryone.info/book/scan.

WEB ACCESSIBILITY AND
THE LAW

IT's important to repeat what we've previously stated: We are not attorneys, and even though we're talking with an attorney in this chapter, we are not providing legal advice. This information is based on our experience in web accessibility and the legal landscape surrounding it as this book releases in spring 2023. If you have questions or believe you need legal advice, please consult with an attorney.

Fair warning: This chapter is likely to scare you as we look at what *could* legally happen if your site isn't accessible. As you read, you'll find that your risk is low, but we want to give you the facts as they currently stand, in particular for those in the United States.

The Global Legal and Legislative Landscape

Around the world, there are various laws related to web accessibility, and those laws often rely on the Web Content Accessibility Guidelines (WCAG) in determining if a website is accessible or not. Generally, these laws seek to regulate government sites and websites that provide public services or that receive government funding.

Outside the U.S., there is often consideration for how large a company is for it to come under the legislation. In countries outside of the U.S. where the web accessibility of commercial websites is legislated, often individuals can't just sue the business, but instead they must go through an administrative process to file a complaint. (As you would for any laws governing your business, make sure you are aware of what applies to you based on where you live.)

In the U.S., there are a myriad of laws for government and public sector websites, as well as industries like air travel.

For websites and other digital properties, though, whether they're run by a large company or an individual, there are no specific laws or regulations to indicate what must be done to make a site accessible, which can make things difficult in the U.S. because of the litigious nature of the country.

In 2022 more than 4,000 lawsuits were filed in the United States related to web accessibility.[1] This number doesn't consider demand letters, which are impossible to track and are designed to get a defendant to settle out of court for a sum of money and the promise to make the site accessible. When factoring in these letters, it's possible the number of overall complaints on web accessibility is substantially higher.

Most web accessibility lawsuits claim that an inaccessible site is a form of discrimination and also cite the Americans with Disabilities Act (ADA), even though the ADA itself doesn't specifically address web accessibility. Around the U.S., the courts are mixed on if a company having a physical location in some way relates to website accessibility.

However, it's important to note that not having a physical

location doesn't protect you from the possibility of receiving a complaint.

A complaint can be against a site that sells goods and doesn't have a physical location or one that has only content. It's simply that those types of sites are targeted far less than ones that also have the physical location connection.

Unfortunately, as we noted, at this point in the U.S., there are few specific laws around digital accessibility, and that has allowed for plaintiffs to make a cottage industry out of filing suits and sending demand letters.

Since the ADA doesn't specifically address websites, the suits and demand letters use various aspects of the ADA, and sometimes state laws, to make the cases.

It's hoped that, eventually, either the U.S. Department of Justice or the U.S. Congress will create specific laws and guidance around web accessibility so it's clear what is required because a site can be accessible for users without meeting every aspect of the Web Content Accessibility Guidelines.

What an Expert Says

Michael Karlin is an associate at The Karlin Law Firm. He's California-based and he has a focus on accessibility law, both physical spaces as well as websites. We routinely consult with Michael as part of our UsableNet work, and we wanted his point of view about how creative entrepreneurs should manage accessibility and how it relates to their businesses.

It bears repeating that Michael is not giving specific legal advice here. If you have questions, please consult with an attorney, preferably one like Michael who has experience in web accessibility.

Is My Site at Risk for a Suit or Demand Letter?

"I haven't seen too much with smaller content creators. The really small mom and pops I've seen hit are still e-commerce-type sites selling physical products or services (like a doctor's office)," says Michael.

He also notes that in these cases, it's e-commerce on the company's website domain, not where a visitor is linked to a site like Amazon, Etsy, eBay, a Payhip or Shopify store, or any site that's on another domain to make the purchase.

Be aware, however, that at this writing, the law isn't entirely clear regarding if you'd be completely safe selling on a site that's on another domain, even though it's the responsibility of that website owner to manage the accessibility.

It's important to make sure you're sending your customers to a digital storefront that is accessible, so as you're selecting an e-commerce platform to work with, take the time to review their accessibility policy. That way you'll know their commitment to accessibility and what kind of experience the customers you send to them can expect.

Remember that you also have the responsibility to ensure the content you add to that site is as accessible as the site allows you to make it, such as using good alternative text on images you upload and using colors that have proper contrast.

The way sites are targeted also helps to lower your risk. "Plaintiffs are just saying, I'm going after 'this industry group today,'" says Michael. "They go on Google and look for 'hamburger restaurants in Santa Monica,' and they just go through the list one by one and quickly run an automated assessment.

"If I Google a generic term like 'author,' I can get a list, but it may not clearly be a list of author's websites, versus a targeted search like 'bike shops in San Diego,' where every result is a website for a bike shop. Content creators become a bunch of small fish in a very large pool. Are they going to sift through all those results? No. You end up being one of a hundred thousand rather than one of fifty."

Don't Be a Target

If you're taking care of the content elements we highlight throughout this book, you're taking the right steps. Michael also has some additional tips on how to minimize your risk.

Fix easy-to-find issues: This is particularly true for your home page because in our experience, if the home page appears to have good accessibility, it's less likely any investigation will go further. "It's a combination of fairly small things, manageable targets, that I think everyone should be doing," Michael says.

Automated scan: Many plaintiffs make their first review of a site using a tool that can scan a page. "I see a large majority of plaintiffs and their attorneys using WAVE because they're not going to spend an hour and a half looking for the littlest error that their screen reader picks up," says Michael. "They want a quick assessment where they just have some number that they can go after and say there were violations."

A scan can only identify a fraction of the problems related to the accessibility of a site, so getting a clean bill of health from a scan doesn't mean your site is fully accessible for all users. However, doing everything you can to ensure your site has no errors that an automated scan can report is a step you can take to lower your legal risk. We discuss running a WAVE scan in the "What Can You Find with an Accessibility Scan" section.

Keyboard navigation: Another simple thing to do is check the keyboard navigation. Can you interact with everything—links, menus, forms, multimedia, etc.—if you're using only a keyboard?

Does tab navigation move through the site in a logical way, from left to right and top to bottom, without jumping around the page? Can you easily find where the focus is because the item is highlighted?

Have an accessibility statement: Michael says that having a statement shows people that you're taking this seriously. That statement must have, at a minimum, an email address where people can contact you if they're having any issues with navigating your site, accessing your content, and, if you have items for sale, making purchases.

Michael also says it's important that when you get an email to that address, you respond as quickly as possible with what the user needs to complete the task they were doing on the site. You should also fix whatever caused the issue.

If you have a larger business and can afford to do so, Michael recommends offering a phone number on the accessibility statement too. Ideally, it would be a toll-free number that could ring your business phone during business hours and have a voicemail box outside of those hours. As your business scales up, it could make sense to have this kind of customer service available.

You can review the simple accessibility statement we use at ContentForEveryone.info/accessibility-statement. You are welcome to use our statement as a template for your own.

Accessible multimedia: If you're creating audio and video content, make them accessible with, at a minimum, transcripts and captions. It's quick and easy to check if there's a correctly edited transcript available or if a video has proper captions. With the available tools in the marketplace, they are also something that everyone can create correctly.

What If I Get a Demand Letter or Suit?

Michael cautions everyone to take any demand or suit you receive seriously and to get in touch with an attorney immediately, preferably one who understands web accessibility complaints. He understands, though, that attorney fees might be more than your business can handle, and while you can try to deal with it on your own, it could also cost more money.

"If you can't afford an attorney to help you out, the success rate isn't great," Michael says. "You're going to be paying a higher amount to settle, or the other side can completely ignore you. You can also try to plead poverty [because the business is so small or is a hobby] but they're not necessarily going to take your word for it."

Realistically, if you end up with a demand or suit, the best advice is to seek professional counsel.

Considering the Risk, Is it Worth it to Have a Website?

The short answer is yes.

"It doesn't make sense to just take your presence out of the internet, because you lose all that value, particularly as a content creator where branding is everything," Michael says. "There is a lot of value in having your own website and you're going to lose that if you just rely on social media as the only thing that's out there for you."

Michael summarizes it this way:

- Get your site as clean and accessible as possible.

- Have any products you're selling available on third party websites.

It's his belief, as mentioned before, that a site that is purely informational, where no products are sold on its domain, is less likely to fall under the purview of the ADA, thus keeping your risk minimal.

CONCLUSION

WE WANT to leave you with the message we gave you in the "What Can You Do?" section.

Progress over perfection.

We can't stress that enough. Unless you're doing nothing, whatever choice you make about creating accessible content isn't wrong.

You can focus on fixing all the content on your website quickly, and that would be wonderful.

You might also take care of only certain types of issues or work only on certain pages.

Your choice might also be to create accessible content going forward and not revisit the past.

Those are all acceptable options.

We've provided you with the information you need to do the work, the benefits for your audience of doing it, and shared the risk (albeit limited risk) on the legal side. Do what's best for your audience, your creative business, and you.

The websites that Jeff runs for his writing and podcasts have evolved over time with most of the content created over the past three years being accessible. However, older content isn't as accessible. He improves older areas as his time and cash flow allow. Would he like to do more and do it faster? Absolutely.

We do ask that you do something. Everyone who creates content on the web has a responsibility to make sure that it's as accessible for everyone as possible. Our hope is that now you know the rules, you can seamlessly use them as you make new content—whether it's words, images, or multimedia.

In addition to creating accessible content yourself, we hope you'll spread the word about doing it too. How you do that can take many forms. Of course, you could tell your creative friends to pick up a copy of this book, which we would appreciate very much.

You can take other actions too. If you find a fellow creator using colors without enough contrast, or communicating only via images, or doing something else you recognize as inaccessible, you can gently let them know the accessible way to do it.

"Gently" is important. We don't believe anyone sets out to make inaccessible content, so it's better to politely educate so others can do better too. The adage "you don't know what you don't know" applies, and you have the opportunity to help teach people about content accessibility who currently don't know about it.

Outside of large companies that have been prompted to make their websites and apps accessible or for those involved in advocacy for people who are disabled, this isn't a topic that's widely discussed. It certainly isn't something that the content, email, and social platforms put front and center.

While there are many accessibility features available, they are rarely highlighted so people can find out about them and use them easily.

We're all in this together, and if we each do our part to make our piece, or pieces, of the web more accessible, everyone will benefit and no one will be left out.

Thank you for reading this book and, hopefully, beginning to do the work. We'd love to know what you're starting to do on your site and in your emails and social posts as a result of what we've told you about here. You can email us at contact@contentforeveryone.info.

Make sure to keep an eye on our website at ContentForEveryone.info. We'll post articles with updates, examples, and more accessibility information.

ACKNOWLEDGMENTS

First and foremost, we want to again thank *you* for picking up
this book and for the efforts you'll take to make your content,
and by extension the web overall, more accessible.

Thanks to our incredible colleagues at UsableNet.
UsableNet is where our passion for digital accessibility
began, and we're excited to bring that passion to the creative
community.

We very much appreciate and thank Joe DiNero, Karla
Hailer, E.M. Lindsey, and Heather Neff for sharing their
experiences on the internet with us. We can tell you all about
the barriers inaccessible content can create, but it resonates
even more when you get stories from someone who must
navigate the barriers every day. We hope you learned from
them just as we did.

This book was improved because of the people who read
it early and provided feedback: author/podcaster Sacha Black,
author services provider Leslie Copeland, author/podcaster
(and Jeff's husband) Will Knauss, and author/podcaster/con-
tent creator Sarah Wendell. Thank you for validating that
what we wrote made sense and letting us know when it
didn't.

We routinely consult with California-based attorney
Michael Karlin. We thank him for taking the time to talk with
us so that we could bring you information about the legal side
of digital accessibility.

Another valuable member of our team we must thank is

our editor Jennifer Smith, who made sure our i's were dotted, t's crossed, and commas were in the right place.

A special shout-out and thanks to our friend and fellow UsableNetter Giacomo Petri, who is far more technical about digital accessibility than we are. His input was invaluable to make sure that while we were keeping things as simple as possible for you, we were also technically correct.

ABOUT THE AUTHORS

Jeff Adams is a Certified Professional in Accessibility Core Competencies (CPACC) by the International Association of Accessibility Professionals (IAAP). As the Accessibility Operations Director for UsableNet, a company focused on making the digital world more accessible and usable, he consults with clients around the world about digital accessibility. In addition, Jeff's a creative entrepreneur as an author and podcaster. You can learn more about his creative endeavors at JeffAdamsWrites.com and BigGayFictionPod cast.com.

Michele Lucchini is the Vice President of Delivery and Accessibility Operations for UsableNet and oversees the teams responsible for ensuring a client's success in their digital accessibility program. Michele has a background rooted in software development and later he moved to team and operation management. Thanks to experience gathered over two decades, Michele is an expert in helping companies, from the largest to the smallest, make their digital experiences accessible.

RESOURCES & REFERENCES

Why Accessible Content Matters

1. "Disability Impacts All of Us," Centers for Disease Control and Prevention: https://www.cdc.gov/ncbddd/disabilityandhealth/info graphic-disability-impacts-all.html
2. Statistic from "Towards an Accessible Canada," Government of Canada: https://www.canada.ca/en/employment-social-development/ programs/accessible-canada.html
3. "Disability Prevalence by Age Group, FYE 2020 to 2021, United Kingdom," Gov.uk: https://www.gov.uk/government/statistics/family-resources-survey-financial-year-2020-to-2021/family-resources-survey-financial-year-2020-to-2021#disability-1
4. "How many persons with disabilities live in the EU?," European Disability Forum: https://www.edf-feph.org/newsroom-news-how-many-persons-disabilities-live-eu/
5. "Disability and Health," World Health Organization: https://www.who.int/news-room/fact-sheets/detail/disability-and-health
6. "Disability Impacts All of Us," Centers for Disease Control and Prevention: https://www.cdc.gov/ncbddd/disabilityandhealth/info graphic-disability-impacts-all.html

Accessing Content on the Web

1. "What is AT?," Assistive Technology Industry Association: https://www.atia.org/home/at-resources/what-is-at/

The Web Content Accessibility Guidelines and What They Mean to You

1. "Web Content Accessibility Guidelines (WCAG) 2 Overview," World Wide Web Consortium (W3C): https://www.w3.org/WAI/standards-guidelines/wcag/

4. Headings

1. "Screen Reader User Survey #9 Results," WebAIM: https://webaim.org/projects/screenreadersurvey9/#finding

8. Audio & Video

1. "Verizon Media and Publicis Media Find Viewers Want Captions," 3PlayMedia: https://www.3playmedia.com/blog/verizon-media-and-publicis-media-find-viewers-want-captions/
2. "How Many People Use Captions and Subtitles?," 3Play Media: https://www.3playmedia.com/blog/who-uses-closed-captions-not-just-the-deaf-or-hard-of-hearing

9. Seizures

1. "Why Do Some Images Cause Seizures While Others Do Not," Medical News Today: https://www.medicalnewstoday.com/articles/317352

What Can You Find with an Accessibility Scan?

1. "WAVE Documentation," WebAIM: https://wave.webaim.org/api/docs?format=html

Web Accessibility and the Law

1. "Five Years of ADA Web and App Lawsuits – Key Observations and Trends," UsableNet: https://blog.usablenet.com/five-years-of-ada-web-and-app-lawsuits-key-observations-and-trends

Made in United States
North Haven, CT
29 January 2025

65132649R00088